A FRESH LOOK
AT THE
NEW TESTAMENT
DEACON

By Dr. John H. Walker, D.Min.

A Fresh Look

at the

New Testament Deacon

By Dr. John H. Walker, D.Min.

Copyright © 2001 Orman Press
ISBN 1-891773-17-8

Printed in the United States of America

DEDICATION

To the deacons of Macedonia Baptist Church in Charlotte, North Carolina, because of their faithful commitment to uphold the pastor's arms and to be pioneers for this *new millennium.*

TABLE OF CONTENTS

ACKNOWLEDGEMENTS

I have been blessed by the many hands that have supported me in the writing of this book. I thank Veronica Briscoe for her typing skills and the analytical reading ability to understand the secret code of my penmanship. I thank Anita Hill for her passion in helping research the material for this book. I thank my wife, Rosie, for her encouragement to continue and persevere in spite of obstacles. I thank her for her love, support and sacrifice. Finally, I want to thank my children, Janetta and John II, for their patience and sacrifices.

FOREWORD

by Reverend George O. McCalep, Jr., Ph.D.

As I travel across this nation lecturing and preaching on church growth and spiritual development, I am bombarded by war stories that mainly relate to broken, unreconciled relationships between deacons and the church, deacons and the trustees, deacons and other deacons, and deacons and the pastor. Most of this conflict could have been prevented if the selection process had been biblical and Holy Spirit led--followed by biblical training and a clever biblical understanding of rules and responsibilities.

Dr. Walker's book, *A Fresh Look at the New Testament Deacon*, is written in the context of the traditional Black Church and will go a long way toward solving this perpetual conflict. Dr. Walker has carefully crafted, in these pages, the role of the pastor in contrast and compared to the role of the deacon. An emphasis is put on a biblical relationship between the pastor and deacon that results in an effective deacon's ministry. The deacon is viewed as a servant to a servant and a partner with a servant in the role of ministry. Dr. Walker deals straightforwardly on the issue of authority in the church.

Embedded within the major thrust of the book are gems of

wisdom relative to leadership qualification, preparation and skills. Dr. Walker's formal training, and leadership and pastoral experience adds tremendous credibility to the book. I highly recommend it and plan to incorporate it into the deacon's training curriculum at Greenforest Community Baptist Church, where I am blessed to pastor. This book is, without a doubt, a must read for all pastors and deacons.

INTRODUCTION

There is a critical problem concerning the deacons and the local church, and State and National Baptist Conventions. The deacons are assuming leadership roles without being equipped for the task of leadership. The relationship between the pastor and deacon is widening because there is a misunderstanding concerning the mission of the church, pastoral leadership and the role of the deacons.

Traditionally, pastors have failed to equip the laity with the necessary tools for leadership. One of the reasons there has been little equipping in the African American Baptist Church is because of the low educational level of the black clergy. There was a time when black pastors were among some of the most educated men in the community.[1] However, that day has come and gone. This is the age of the educational specialist. The pastor/teacher is to be a well-oriented teaching specialist. The pastor must prepare himself for the task of feeding and equipping the flock. This will involve taking advantage of every teaching opportunity that he may find to provide the word of truth.

The pastor's failure to equip has created a vacuum within the ranks of leadership in the local church. The pastor has failed to recognize that the Holy Spirit has equipped church members to do the work of the ministry. The pastor's challenge is to **discover, enlist** and **utilize** the resources that are available.[2]

Every believer is indwelt and baptized by the Holy Spirit at the moment of conversion. The believer is commanded to be continually filled with the Holy Spirit. This Spirit-filled life is the normal life intended for every Christian. Then the Holy Spirit empowers the church for ministry. In His sovereignty and omniscience, He gives a variety of gifts to the church so that each believer may use them to build up the family of God. Pastors and laity should rejoice in the love, joy, peace, and power the Holy Spirit has given, and the church should not blaspheme by attributing His work to the devil; nor should the church quench the Holy Spirit by trying to restrict Him to traditional patterns. The contemporary Christian Church should not feel threatened by the Holy Spirit but should recognize that He is the indispensable One. Apart from the ministry of the Holy Spirit, there can be no true and lasting revitalization of the church.

Every Christian desiring to be useful and effective in Christian service should ask, "What are my spiritual gifts?" There are a number of tests that may be applied to determine these gifts. **First**, there should be a desire for a particular gift. **Second**, the gift should be identified and utilized for the work of the kingdom. Also, gifts will be discovered while in operation. As service is performed, the results will indicate whether a particular gift is actually present. Another test is whether others recognize the presence of a gift. Once a gift is discovered, the person should strive to develop it. Individuals should be placed in positions of service in which they can exercise their spiritual gifts.

The church can never make a desperately needed impact upon the world until individual Christians begin to utilize, in the power of the resurrected Lord, the gifts God has given the church. Little progress can be made as long as church members feel that a minister can be hired to exercise all gifts while the laymen merely listen to and pay him. Church leaders must avoid exploiting the talents of the congregation rather than helping them find their spiritual gifts. The "value" of the Christian life will be determined by the degree to which Christians make use of the gifts that God has given them. God chooses His workers based on what they can become rather than on what they are at the present time.

Two chapters in the Bible form the basis for study: 1 Corinthians 12 and Ephesians 4. They describe how God provides spiritual ennoblement beyond natural ability and thus makes provision for the progress of His work.

In Ephesians 4:12-13, Paul reveals the purposes of spiritual gifts:

> To prepare God's people for works of service, so that the body of Christ may be built up until we all reach unity in the faith and in the knowledge of the Son of God and become mature, attaining the full measure of perfection found in Christ. (NIV)

Spiritual gifts perfect, mend and complete the saints, causing them to serve more effectively. The ultimate purpose of the gifts is the building up of the body of Christ.[3]

One can readily see the importance of helping people discover their gifts and realize their unique importance early. These gifts assure their worth to individuals. It must be remembered, however, that there is no such thing as receiving a gift solely for one's own personal use and edification. The nature of the gift, whatever it may be, is such that it should be used to build up the body of Christ. The pastor/teacher's task is to help every believer know what his gifts are and to utilize them for the well-being of the church. The church is actually handicapped if any member's gifts are not being properly applied. **The pastor must be careful that he does not exhaust himself in work detail, depriving others in the body of Christ from exercising their gifts and responsibilities in the ministry of the church.**

Enlistment is critical when equipping the laity for Christian leadership. For too long the church has **enlisted** persons into leadership positions who have not met the basic spiritual qualification: salvation. This qualification may not be considered essential for leadership in the business world, but it is absolutely imperative for work in the cause of Christ. No one can satisfactorily serve a church if he does not have the inner resources and deep personal experience with Christ to interpret His message to others. This plan of enlistment depends upon the Lord's help and leadership.[4] Without the guidance of the Holy Spirit, there is no guarantee of success. Throughout the enlistment process for leadership, "pray without ceasing" (1 Thessalonians 5:17).

Unfortunately, there are some individuals serving in leadership roles today who are not spiritual and have no idea what they are supposed to be doing. Many are in positions because of their social and economic ties with the church. The pastor/teacher must enlist only those who are willing to be taught. The pastor/teacher must utilize the resources God has given to the church. The local church has lost many members because unless they could personally benefit the pastor and his administration, they were never used within the church structure. The pastor must be aware that if an individual is fresh out of the world of sin, and brand new to the state of salvation, they might not be the best person to serve because they are not spiritually mature. Also, laity should not be utilized before (1) they have been taught, (2) their spiritual gifts and abilities have been identified and (3) they have had an opportunity to share in the vision of the church.[5]

Deacons have assumed a role of responsibility that has never been given to them. This causes contention and strife, and has led the deacon to believe that he has influence and power that the pastor must recognize. Historically, in the Black Church, the deacon was looked upon as the church's overlord and not a spiritual shepherd. The problem has extended itself to these modern times in which we live. In the average black church, the deacon board is the power board.[6] Rev. R. L. White, in his book *The Preacher Deacon Dilemna,* clearly states that shortly after slavery, when black congregations began to grow, an overwhelming need arose for good preachers. This period was called the Shortage of Preachers' period, and it gave rise to what was known as the circuit-riding preacher. In order to service as many communities as possible, a preacher would pastor four churches--preaching at one each Sunday. (Even today there are still once-a-month churches, mostly in rural areas.) During this era, the pastor lived a long distance from the church he pastored. The deacons took care of any problems that would arise during the month (with the exception of death within the church family). If the preacher was scheduled to come for Sunday service, the deacons had church conference the Friday or Saturday before the meeting day. It was typical for the preacher, during these times, to say to the deacons, "Y'all fix it, and whatever you do is alright with me." Over a period of time, the deacons began to feel that it was their job to run the church and the preacher's job was to do the preaching. The preacher began to take on the image of a hired hand. The parishioners accepted this arrangement, and the office of the deacon began to take on more and more power. Because of the lack of training and teaching, the average church member did not understand that each member had a legitimate vote in the decision-making of the church. The deacons then, in effect, began to control the church. Over several generations, this practice began to take on a life of its own and became a perceived institution common in the Baptist Church.[7]

In later years, as ministers increased in number and became better educated, they began fulfilling the role of pastor in ways other than preaching. The preacher demanded more of a role in the administration of church affairs. The deacons felt he had begun to trespass on their "turf" and resisted the change that the more modern preacher tried to institute. This has resulted in an unholy war between the pastor and deacons. At the root of the problem is a misunderstanding of roles and responsibilities because no one was required to engage in pre-ministry training. Pastors believe that the power should be in their hands. It is this kind of misunderstanding that sets up the type of spiritual warfare that has resulted in the downfall of many churches.[8]

The twenty-first century pastor must take a new approach to leadership, equipping the deacons by teaching them about the task of leadership.[9] The church ought to require some minimum standards for their leaders. If preachers have requirements that they must fit, no deacon should be let off the hook. Leadership skills, manner of life, Bible beliefs, attitudes about pastoral authority and congregational policy should be examined before any individual is installed in office.[10] People agree with the concept that the pastor should be biblically fit for leadership. However, people bring different perspectives to a position of leadership when it's their time to lead. Pastors should take a stand against such nonsense and let people know unequivocally that there are no exceptions to the biblical mandates for qualified leadership.

The pastor must become secure enough in his calling to not feel threatened by educated, qualified laypersons. The pastor must be conscious of his own sense of being. He must know who he is, whose he is and why he is called to pastor. The pastor's identity must be God-given and not people-defined.[11] Members must be encouraged and given opportunities to become participants at every level of church activity.[12] In order for members to function in the kind of leadership roles that our Lord intended for His church, the training and direction for ministry in the local church must come from the God-anointed pastor/teacher that the Holy Spirit has placed over the congregation.[13]

God has permitted the church to have pastoral assistants, aides, associates and deacons. These persons were never intended to lead the pastor or alter the pastor's plans. They were to share in the implementation of what God has called the pastor to do.

The world is filled with followers, supervisors and managers, but few leaders. Leadership is like beauty: it is hard to define but easy to recognize. Time has produced a legacy of distinguished and outstanding individuals who have impacted history and the ongoing development of mankind. These individuals were both men and women, rich and poor, learned and unlearned, trained and untrained. They came from every race, color, language and culture of the world. Many of them had no ambition to become great leaders. Most of the individuals who have greatly affected mankind were simple people called by circumstances that demanded the hidden qualities of their character--they were driven by a personal, passionate goal.[14]

Leaders are ordinary people who accept (or are placed under) extraordinary circumstances that bring out their latent potential, producing a character that inspires the confidence and trust of others. The church is in desperate need of deacons. I would suggest that in the twenty-first century, we are at a confluence of historic tides. In the past two decades, a relatively short span of time within this century, the world has experienced remarkable changes in the realms of science, technology, medicine, space, and even in the church. Strangely, this century has also seen more distressing times than any previous century--wars, monstrous new weapons, countless natural disasters and fatal diseases.[15]

This generation lives in a swirling tide of events, dreams, promises, threats and changing ideas about the present and future. This century has been the most politically interesting, the bloodiest, the most revolutionary and the most unpredictable of any century in history. This confluence of conditions presses this generation to ask, anew, "Why am I here? What is the purpose of life? Why are life and reality the way they are?"[16]

The leaders of our time are bewildered when they are called upon to explain the reasons for the present morass or to suggest a direction for the future. The trepidation is to maintain the status quo. Competent leaders are needed at this juncture. Added to this bleak perspective is the painful reality that over the past few decades, the world seems to have experienced a dramatic leadership vacuum.[17] In every arena--political, civic, economic, social and spiritual--there is an absence of effective, quality leadership; and recent events indicate that our current generation has failed to prepare for effective leadership for the future.

The Christian enterprise--the church, the home and the school--is desperately in need of leaders. Within the Black Baptist Church there is a dire need for qualified leadership.[18] There is undue stress upon both the pastor and people. The leadership within many congregations has not had any leadership or biblical training, which creates a climate for contention and ill-defined roles. There is confusion as to who is in charge and, consequently, the Baptist Church operates as a democracy. The leadership controls the church by making sure that the pastor is submissive and receives authority from the deacons. Others argue that the deacons are rightfully in charge because pastors come and go and are therefore transient. This attitude usually results in board-run organizations that are impenetrable because the deacons have a difficult time relinquishing authority that was never theirs in the first place. This situation leads to a dysfunctional church.[19] When the church is dysfunctional, leadership problems are inevitable.

Empowering the laity is crucial to change. The concept of "pray, pay and obey" is painfully evident as the primary perceived function of laypeople. But the laity are valuable because of who they are and what they can do. The laity is not being used to achieve the goals of the church--they are the goal. The future awaits the response of the church--a future that will not tolerate yesterday's church in today's world, let alone the world of tomorrow. The laity must be equipped and released for ministry.

The local church is facing a critical hour. Presently, twenty percent of the membership is doing eighty percent of the church's work. This means overworking some, while the great majority of the congregation does little. According to Floyd Massey, Jr. and Samuel Berry McKinney, authors of *Church Administration in the Black Perspective,* only about four in ten members of any congregation are involved in the ministry of the church. Either by design or decision, the majority have been told (and taught) to sit down while the pastor and deacons stand and do the Lord's work for them. A wise pastor will not try to be all things to all people at all times. A wise pastor will serve effectively and efficiently when he understands that his task is not to do the work of the church but to equip the members of Christ (the church).[20]

Having served as a pastor for more than thirteen years, and having preached and taught for over nineteen years, I have been afforded the opportunity to influence the denomination. I am acquainted with the problem of deacon leadership. The Macedonia Baptist Church of Charlotte, Inc., has been a change agent in the area of deacon leadership. There is a spirit of empowerment and mutual respect that exists between the pastor and deacon.

I believe the empowerment of laity can be furthered in the denomination if deacons are equipped in comprehensive leadership programs for laity, and if a climate of mutual respect can be developed between pastor and deacon. This will clarify roles and solidify the mission of the church. The primary objective of this book is to invoke a fresh look at the New Testament deacon and to develop a biblical relationship with pastors and deacons. Deacons who embrace the pastor's vision can help the congregation catch his vision as well. When such a relationship exists, the church will be more harmonious and the pastor will be grateful that he has men and women who want to make the ministry productive.

CHAPTER ONE

THE NEW TESTAMENT DEACON

The words deacon, <u>dek'n</u>, deaconess, <u>dekines</u>, and the term <u>olakoros</u>, <u>diakonos</u>, and its cognates occur many times in the New Testament; as do its synonyms uparatas, huperetes, and <u>hureks</u>, <u>doulos</u>, with their respective cognates. In general, the terms denote the service or ministration of the bondservant (<u>doulos</u>), underling (<u>huperetes</u>) or helper (<u>diakonos</u>), in all shades and graduations of meaning, both literal and metaphorical.[21]

Many have sought the origin of the diaconate in the institution of the seven at Jerusalem (Acts 6), and this view was echoed by many of the church fathers. The seven were appointed to serve tables in order to permit the twelve to continue steadfastly in prayer and in the ministry of the word. The word deacon (<u>diakonos</u>) means one who is a servant or bondservant appointed to carry out the orders given to him, as an assistant helper, not only in waiting on tables, but whatever duties are given to him by the apostle/pastor.[22] A New Testament church is made up of saved people who have been joined by the Holy

Spirit into the body of Christ. The body is composed of three designations of members: "... To all the saints in Christ Jesus which are in Philippi, with the bishops and deacons" (Philippians 1:1). The church is made up of saints, shepherds, and servants. The saints are the saved people. "Saints" is a term commonly used in the New Testament to refer to Christian believers. It does not mean that a person is sinless. It is never applied to a person as part of his name, such as Saint John.

The shepherds are the pastors of the churches. They are called shepherds because their work is to guide and provide spiritual nourishment for the flock. The servants are the deacons of the churches. Their title (diakonos) means "one who serves." Deacon is the title given to one whose primary ministry is to serve. It is not as much the title to an office as it is the description of a ministry. It is to be used to describe the lifestyles of individuals who have been set apart by the church to serve the congregation. Although the seven brethren designated to serve the church in Acts Chapter 6 are not called deacons, their ministry mirrored that of men who filled the office.

In the days of the early church, there were no public welfare systems available to care for widows and helpless children. They took care of their own.

> Neither was there any among then that lacked; for as many as were possessors of land or houses sold them, and brought the prices of the things that were sold and laid them down at the apostle's feet and distribution was made unto every man according as he had need. (Acts 4:34, 35)

The Jews had a great reputation for their welfare work with widows and the poor. When the Jews became followers of Christ, they continued to practice what they were accustomed to. In the synagogue there was a routine custom: two collectors went around the market and private houses every Friday morning and made collection for the needy--partly in money and partly in goods. Later in the day, the money was distributed. Those who were temporarily in need received enough to enable them to carry on, and those who were permanently unable to support themselves received enough for fourteen meals (enough for two meals a day for the ensuring week).

Deacons of today must never stand in the way of giving to meet the needs of the poor. The church has been given the responsibility of meeting the needs of people and the needs within the church; the deacon has the mission of ministering to those needs. The deacon's mission is in today's society. If he fulfills his mission, God's objective will be met. The deacon has been commissioned fruit--first as a Christian and second as a deacon--in order to minister to the needs of God's people under the leadership of the pastor. Deacons do not operate from out of the covering of their pastor.

The Apostle Peter said that it didn't make sense to leave the word of God to serve tables or to minister to all the other needs of the people (Acts 6:2). This did not mean that they would no longer minister to them; rather, it was a matter of priority. Their number one responsibility was to proclaim the Gospel. Since the church had grown to approximately 50,000 disciples, they needed help. So the Apostles, with the church's assistance, appointed deacons. The deacons were called to reinforce the work that the Apostles had previously done, and not try to replace them in the work. They were co-laborers sharing the same vision as the Apostles.

The deacon must never be in competition with the pastor. Neither the pastor nor the deacon can function in total success without the other. Yes, one may be able to do some good things without the other, but the service of ministering to people will never reach its full potential until pastor and deacon work as a team. According to Ephesians 4:11-16 and Acts 6:2, the pastor's role is to **(1) minister the word**, **(2) equip the saints** to do the work of the ministry, and **(3) pray for the saints**. The pastor trains the deacons to wait on and take care of the saints. Deacons take care of the small matters; they take the larger ones to the pastor. God designed this divine dependency, and neither party can ever become self-sufficient. Who is in charge? Who is superior (rank)? Who is running the church? These questions should never become an issue; and if they do, a demonic spirit has entered in to the relationship and it must be rebuked. Remember, Jesus is the owner of the church; Jesus is the head of his church; and the Holy Spirit runs the church. When the pastor and deacon work as a team in the ministry, great work can be accomplished.

The Prerequisites of Deaconship

I believe that for too long in our churches, we have put too much emphasis on qualification and not enough on divinely inspired investigation. We take for granted that the individual who seems to be qualified has everything in order. For instance, has the potential deacon ever invited Christ into his/her life as personal Lord and Savior, or did he/she simply join the church? Salvation is about joining Christ and the kingdom of God, not the church. Joining the church ought to be the result of joining Christ. We who are looking out among ourselves to find individuals for this work must take the approach that we cannot substitute or sidestep the essentials. According to Dr. Wayne Goodwin, a professor at Gordon Conwell Theological Seminary,

Charlotte, NC, any individual striving for Christian leadership must consider the paradigm of "being, becoming, doing."

The **prerequisites of leadership** focus on the "being of a leader." **First**, deacons must know that their salvation is the foundation for Christian leadership. Christians must have a Christ-centered life. Therefore, a prerequisite of leadership must be the acceptance of Jesus Christ as their Savior and Lord. **Second**, deacons must exemplify a biblical faith that God is setting them apart and working through them. Deacons must be challenged to explore their true "being," which is of the heart-- the inner self. An "I and Thou" relationship is established with Christ. This quality is essential in the formation of potential leaders. Leadership is not born but cultivated. Spending quality time with God will allow gifts to surface.

Christian leaders must understand basic fundamentals of the Christian faith, such as spiritual character, maturity and faithfulness. From the period of the early church, leaders were set apart to carry out the various ministries of the church. Paul wisely wrote the Corinthian church that there are varieties of services, but the same God (1 Corinthians 12:4, 5). The believer's gifts will be identified when he focuses on his being. "And God has appointed in the church first apostles, second prophets, third teachers, then workers of miracles, then healers, helpers, administrators, speakers in various kinds of tongues" (1 Corinthians 12:28, RSV). The church at its best has understood that every person is called into ministry and that no one's work is downgraded. Every believer is called to serve the Lord with his being. The believer's identity begins with God. Christian identity begins with God, an upward focus and a vertical dimension.

Henri Noumen, author of *The Wounded Healer*, emphasizes the self-giving aspect of the spiritual formation of the priest as the hard and often painful process of self-emptying and creating that inner space where the spirit can manifest itself.[23] A person's spiritual formation flows from an understanding of the "being," and character of God.

Goodwin suggests that an excellent way of challenging one-self and gaining a deeper understanding of one's being is by answering the following questions: What do you dream about, cry about, sing about, live for; what will you die for?[24] There must be time for one to experience, enjoy, understand and exercise the new being. *The New Being*, written by Paul Tillich, says that in sermon citing, Christianity is the message of the new creation, the new being, the new reality that has come with the appearance of Jesus, who, for this reason alone, is called the Christ.[25] Jesus is the true example of leadership, for He was a servant leader. Leaders lead by example. Spiritual leaders that inspire the heart ("being") of others can "do."

The **preparation of leadership** focused on "becoming a leader." This process involves nurturing the spirit man. Deacons are more secure and motivated when their pastor believes in them, encourages them, shares with them and trusts them. This nurturing process involves more than encouragement; it also includes modeling. The modeling process is most effective when a leader chooses a model to emulate and then becomes a model to other team members. Nurturing, or becoming, takes time. Becoming provides a Christian with a sense of God's calling.

Deacons realize that in becoming, every call is a call to prepare. Traditionally in Christian circles, persons are "called to the ministry," as Samuel was called to be a prophet and Paul an apostle; this is the divine nature of Christian vocation. A theocentric experience will help one respond to God's will for his life.

According to Richard H. Niebuhr, author of *The Purpose of*

the Church and its Ministry, there are four distinct calls: the call to be a Christian, the secret call, the providential call and the ecclesiastical call.

The Call to Be a Christian
Every Christian has a calling and a vocation under God. The ministry of the deacon is rightly conveyed here as an expression of faith.

The Secret Call
One may answer the call to be set apart in ministry by inwardly becoming aware that God has placed a particular calling on one's life for full-time ministry. This awareness is tested against the calls of other servants in the church and is nurtured through prayer and reflection. Some persons do not have dramatic calls, like the Apostle Paul and the Prophet Samuel, but experience steady growth and higher levels of commitment because there is a constant focus on being. The call to ministry is about being.

The Providential Call
The providential call deals with the relationship between the needs of the church and the society which one wants to meet through the ministry, and through one's own talent and ability. It is not enough for ministry candidates to have a secret call--that call should be tested against an investigation of the person's abilities and the needs of the church. It is about being where the church must begin.

The Ecclesiastical Call
The candidate for church vocation answers the call of a specific congregation or group. The call to service makes no

connection until one is set apart by a congregation, granted a license to preach and has administered the sacraments, as well as met the discipline of church orders.[26] Motives for ministry are many and varied, but can usually be classified as either self-affirming or self-becoming. These motives can be identified and focused on during the early stages of one's consideration and/or acceptance of the vocation. People want to know who they are but feel they cannot discover themselves outside of a social group.[27] A Christian cannot know and appreciate who he is until he has an appreciation of his being. Christian leaders are always in a state of becoming. The quest for everyone that recognizes Jesus is Lord is to build up the Body. The paradigm "becoming" focuses on the inward, while being is focused on the upward. This is the nurturing framework of the Christian. During nurturing, a person accepts his gifts.[28]

The christo-centric community is matured and empowered when the experience of being is ordered and nurtured in a structural environment.[29] The church is primarily and fundamentally a body designed to find expression through each unique individual member. The Holy Spirit equips every member of the Body with gifts designed to express that life. Once a person becomes fully aware that God has uniquely equipped him with spiritual gifts, he is able to become.

The church is empowered and nurtured to help believers become. Becoming is a process of spiritual formation and maturity. The Holy Spirit makes and keeps the church. The church is a community defined by its faith in Christ and by its function as the agent of the Holy Spirit. It is Christ who provides the church with servant leaders to help believers become. The Apostle Paul expected church members to be complete (or become) in knowledge and competence. The local church should provide every opportunity for members to be nurtured.

Believers are saved for an experience of growth in the present. As a familiar hymn puts it, "Love so amazing, so divine, demands my soul, my life, my all."[30] But gifts such as these cannot be given only once; they must constantly be renewed according to the changing circumstances of life. The more persons become, the more they have to offer. Just as salvation is a continuous act of divine grace, the believer's response to it must be a continuous act of divine grace. Therefore, the believer's response to salvation must be a continuous act of human gratitude. The New Testament leaves no doubt that what God wants most is steady growth toward spiritual adulthood, which Paul defined as "the measure of the stature of the fullness of Christ" (Ephesians 4:13). To become Christ-like is the endless challenge of all who owe their existence to the saving intervention of God.

The more persons grow in conformity to the image of God's son (Romans 8:29), the more they share the glory, which is already His by His triumphant exaltation on high. Between the plight from which persons are saved and the purpose for which they are saved stands Jesus Christ as the agent through whom this change is made possible. Neither religion nor philosophy nor morality, valuable as they are, can bring about the process of becoming. Only Christ, who in His earthly life conquered sin, can restore a person to wholeness.

Becoming is sanctification. There are three primary sources of sanctification--upward, inward and outward.[31] These are three routes by which godliness may flow into the believer's life as he experiences the salvific process. When we focus on being, we experience an upward (worship) relationship.

In the Old Testament, certain times and places were set apart as holy so people might gather to worship God. The willingness of God to create a hallowed framework in which worship could occur was in itself proof that God would come to envelop the waiting people with His presence--if they called Him. Central to this experience in the New Testament was the ministry of the word--understood primarily as the word which Jesus brought to reveal God. Jesus was the word of God, and he declared that He gave the disciples God's word. He then prayed that the Father would sanctify them in the truth. Jesus declared, "Thy word is truth." The living and active word of God (Hebrews 4:12) enters our lives and lodges there; it mediates the purpose of God (of whom it speaks)--the God who provokes becoming! The inward source is the **Holy Spirit.**[32] God comes to persons through worship and the spirit of holiness, by which Christ was raised from the dead. The Christian life is a process of working together with the indwelling Spirit of God.

The outward source is **Fellowship** (the experience of koinonia--rich, interactive fellowship).[33] The church is a place where individual believers "pool" their spiritual resources for the good of one another. The holiness of the Corinthians (1 Corinthians 1:2) consisted not in their personal piety but in the richness of the spiritual gifts that they received from God by virtue of their common fellowship with the Son, Jesus Christ. Fellowship (koinonia) means that each is to share his or her experience of God with others.[34]

When Paul said "God made" Christ Jesus "our sanctification" (1 Corinthians 1:30), He meant that the possibility of becoming holy was established as a divine gift, entirely apart from doing or deserving. Ultimately, because the Son of God was the perfect embodiment of holiness, every believer may be sanctified in Christ Jesus. One's acquired holiness is planted at the core of his being before he does anything to make himself holy.

God shapes and molds His servants as they become. Deacons then realize that in becoming, a nurturing process occurs which allows them to accept and utilize their gifts under the guidance of the Holy Spirit. Being is an "I-Thou" relationship; whereas, becoming is an "I-We" relationship.

The **practice of leadership** focuses primarily on the "Doing as a Leader." Deacons must understand the four principles of Christian leadership: Faithfulness, high standards, leading by example and inspiring cooperation from the heart. There is always a great need for qualified laypersons to serve in leadership roles. Remembering that leaders will be held to higher standards than non-leaders, Christ must be the authority and the motivator. As Christians, they utilize their God-given talents in the area of ministry in which they are called. Students were taught that "doing as a leader" requires outreach while utilizing gifts.

Much of what happens in the local church does not have anything to do with the mission of the church. If doing is going to be a response to one's being, one must be aligned with the mission of the church. Purpose and goals--conscious or unconscious--largely determine the direction of one's life and whether one finds freedom and fulfillment as an individual or as a member of the human family. Bishop Bruce P. Blake in an article in the *U.M. Reporter* states, "One of the difficulties with discernment is that when Christians discover God's work, we are tempted to celebrate and praise God, but fail to act in response to our discovery." Discernment and doing cannot be separated. To discern without doing produces apathy. To do without discerning produces occasion for irresponsibility. One must be before one can do, and when one's doing reflects irresponsible behavior, one is in need of a transformation.[35]

The great commission in Matthew 28:19-20 is still alive

today, and the organized church is a significant means for fulfilling Christ's commission. The commission is to make disciples who are characterized by their obedience to the commands of Jesus Christ. The power for fulfilling the command to make disciples was made clear in the restatement of the great commission in Acts 1:8: "But you will receive power when the Holy Spirit comes on you, and you will be my witnesses in Jerusalem, and in all Judea and Samaria, and to the ends of the earth." Only with the power of the spirit can the work of Christ be fulfilled. Power comes with "being," and where there is "being" and a focus on the upward, then ministering to the uninitiated can be effective.

Christians will grow much faster if factors that enhance and encourage spiritual growth are present. The Apostle Paul emphasizes that **(1)** the unity of the faith and **(2)** the knowledge of the Son of God are two key factors that lead to spiritual growth and development. These, he says, will lead to mature manhood, the measure of the stature of the fullness of Christ (Ephesians 4:13). The unity of the faith is the shared understanding, in the church, of the great truths revealed in the Scriptures. Although the Scriptures are unchanging, new light is continually shed through individual prophets and teachers who are given new insights by the Holy Spirit. However, they must be widely shared in the Body, or no new truths will be given (or realized) in the life of the believer. New Christians grow when they exert themselves to understand the Scriptures and when they receive the help of teachers and leaders within the body of Christ. No growth toward wholeness and perfection can occur without this increase in the unity of the faith through the understanding of Christian doctrine. This can only be accomplished by increasing the knowledge of the Son of God. Spiritual development occurs by having a growing encounter with the Lord

Jesus Christ Himself, not just knowing about God, but knowing God, directly and personally. This is a necessary prerequisite for "doing."

This encounter occurs when the knowledge of the faith (hearing) is put into practice (doing). Hearing and doing go hand-in-hand. One cannot fully know Jesus Christ until one follows him. Following Christ is a joy, therefore, "doing should be a joyful response to our being."[36] God desires a whole-hearted, enthusiastic commitment to doing His will. He does not want average Christians. He does not want average missionaries. He wants men and women of God who are sold out to Him; this is not average.

The Christian's doing will be a spring which flows out of a relationship with God. James said, "Draw near to God and He will draw near to you" (James 4:8). Drawing near to God manifests one's being, out of which flows doing. The paradigms of being, becoming and doing are ways of understanding the process of how a sinner is transformed into a saint and commissioned to fulfill God's will in the church and in his personal walk with God.

A Saved Person

A saved person is one that has accepted "God's Plan of Salvation" as truth and has been reconciled (become a new creature) with God through Jesus Christ. 2 Corinthians 5:17, 18 says:

> Therefore if any man be in Christ, he is a new creature: old things are passed away; behold, all things are become new, and all things are of God, who hath reconciled us to himself by Jesus Christ, and

hath given to us the ministry of reconciliation.

Unless one has become a new creature in Jesus Christ himself, he certainly cannot lead others to Christ. Not only should one have accepted "God's Plan of Salvation" for his life, but also know and understand it so he can share it with others. SALVATION means redemption, deliverance and liberation, and being rescued and preserved from destruction. A more practical word is "saved." GOD had a plan to save mankind, even before He made him. In God's wisdom, he knew man would sin so he planned to save him before He formed him out of the dust and blew the breath of life into him. One may wonder why God would make man, in spite of knowing he would sin. God is love, and love must have a recipient. In other words, God needed something or someone to give his love to.

John 3:16 demonstrates God activating his love for mankind's sake: "For God so loved the world that he gave his only begotten son, that whosoever believes in him should not perish, but have everlasting life." Whosoever believes in Jesus shall be saved--Jesus saves. What does Jesus save us from? Satan, Sin and Self. The evidence of being saved is not being controlled by Satan, sin or self, but rather by the Holy Spirit.

A Student of the Holy Word

2 Timothy 2:15 instructs us to review, inspect, examine, mull over, pour over, and meditate over the word of God so we will be able to dissect and/or expound correctly the divine message for ourselves and others. By doing this, we are able to show ourselves acceptable to God without guilt (not being misled or misleading others). Because of this command, the potential deacon must have more than a casual knowledge of God's word.

The Holy Bible records the history of the Hebrew people and of God revealing himself in their lives, as individuals and as a nation. Also, words of wisdom and counsel are there for guidance. The revelation of God through Christ is there to bring the individual back after the separation caused by sin. The story of the early church and the lives of the early Christians has been recorded for encouragement, guidance, instruction and inspiration. The life and work of the deacon demand that casual reading be replaced by planned, dedicated study. Needless to say, one must find meaning in (and for) his own life before he can show someone else meaning in theirs. The Holy Bible is the ultimate authority on life and what God expects of us as individuals.

A Person of Prayer

The potential deacon must practice unceasing prayer in order to be able to find the fullness of the Christian life for himself and to become a leader among the people. Prayer is the avenue for man to communicate with God, and God with man. In prayer he can discover, for himself, God's glory and will. Knowing God's will for his life and for the lives of His people is a must. I cannot imagine anyone trying to lead God's people without God's direction/instruction. That would be like going to a strange land without a map, and not receiving any information (beforehand) relating to the layout of the land. Furthermore, only God knows what his people really need, and when they need it. Sometimes we have desires of the heart but don't really know what we need or what is best for us.

Again, only God knows what his people need, according to his will and plan. Needless to say, God will not give this information to anyone that does not have a close relationship with Him. One cannot keep a close relationship without communicating. (Prayer is the method of communicating with God). We keep our relationship with God intact through prayer, which consists of the following: (1) praising and giving God's name reverence; (2) giving thanks for God's goodness; (3) asking for God's forgiveness of our sins; (4) interceding for others; (5) asking God for his direction, guidance and will for our lives; (6) asking God to supply our needs. Communicating with God on a consistent basis is a must for the deacon.

An Active Worshipper

Worship experiences are an essential in the life of the potential deacon. In his personal relationship with God and as a leader in his home, worship plays an important role: it gives each member of the family the opportunity to grow personally. Public worship provides the privilege of participation in a corporate adventure with God, and communion with him in the most favorable surroundings and with those who, like us, seek a worship experience. The worship experience serves to strengthen us and our faith so that we may endure life--while simultaneously giving God his praise, glory and honor. Remember, as praises go up, blessings come down.

A Tither

God gives only one plan of finance in the Bible, and that is, tithes and offerings from his people. The tithe is the tenth, meaning that God's people are to bring a tenth of their income to the Lord and His work. Offerings are the amounts that are given above the tenth.

God's plan is that every Christian give a gift each Sunday, that gifts be given in proportion to one's income and that gifts be given in a spirit of gladness. "UPON THE FIRST DAY OF

THE WEEK LET EVERYONE OF YOU LAY BY HIM IN STORE, AS GOD HATH PROSPERED HIM" (1 Corinthians 16:2, *emphasis added*). "SO LET HIM GIVE, NOT GRUDGINGLY, OR OF NECESSITY: FOR GOD LOVETH A CHEERFUL GIVER" (2 Corinthians 9:7, *emphasis added*). It is inconceivable that one would not give or, for that matter, give grudgingly. To not give is disobedience--plain and simple. And the one that gives in the wrong spirit loses twice: (1) loses the money and (2) gets no credit from God for the gift. Furthermore, it all belongs to God; he only lends it to us for our good and use. Psalm 24:1 makes it very clear that "THE EARTH IS THE LORD'S AND THE FULNESS THEREOF; THE WORLD, AND THEY THAT DWELL THEREIN" (*emphasis added*). Nothing in this world truly belongs to us--not even ourselves. We belong to Him through creation and redemption. Acceptance of this Scripture as truth should encourage us to demonstrate his love, appreciation and obedience to God by giving back to Him.

The purpose of the tithe is to bless the giver. "IT IS MORE BLESSED TO GIVE THAN TO RECEIVE" (Acts 20:35, *emphasis added*). Giving according to God's plan saves the giver from greed and covetousness. It builds in him a spirit of concern and generosity. The purpose of the tithe is also to bring good into the world. It is a weekly investment in the spiritual welfare of the world. It is your personal effort to halt the progress of infidelity and sin.

While tithing is not to be engaged in by law, in the strict Old Testament sense, it is to be remembered that Jesus expressed his approval of it (Matthew 23:23). That very fact should make it obligatory in our lives. Jesus' express wish should be looked upon, to the Christian, as binding. Tithing, like love, is a natural expression of a Christian's attitude and experience.

In summary, the prerequisites aren't just for the potential

deacon's life, but also for others. The one that will potentially serve in this capacity must lead by example. In every facet of Christian living, the deacon should try to live as an example of the "new person in Jesus Christ."

CHAPTER TWO

WHO, THEN, CAN BE A DEACON?

The diaconate is a God-given ministry, and only the individuals called and/or directed by the Holy Spirit to do this ministry should be deacons. I must clarify the word "called" as it relates to the deacon. One's spirit must bear witness with the pastor's when asked or nominated or appointed to serve. To be appointed to serve in this most important office isn't just left up to our own choosing--or to others--but rather to God himself.

In light of many traditional churches, the question is, "Who, then, can be a deacon?" The qualifications are outlined according to 1 Timothy 3. An individual must meet the biblical prerequisites, have the desire to serve in ministry and, most importantly, be called by God.

I believe we must take a fresh look at who can be a deacon by redefining the roles that exist in most of our churches. Traditionally, only men have served in the role of the deacon. The word deacon means servant; therefore, how can one gender servanthood? Are we going to continue to place value on individuals based solely on gender? We have traditionally placed deacons' wives (and women) in the position of deaconess because of their husbands. I have no problem with deaconesses if, in our traditional church, we would not cheapen the qualifications and class their ministry on a lower level. A deaconess is a female deacon. The deacon and deaconess have the same function and ministry. They both have the unique responsibility of taking care of God's people. The only true difference between deacon and deaconess is gender.[37] The female deacon's ordination should be the same as the male deacon's. To ordain means to put in order, appoint, enlist or authorize officially (as by the lying on of hands). Traditionally, under no circumstance would the deaconess be ordained. The deaconess may have participated in the ordination ceremony, but she was not ordained. She may have been set aside and authorized for a specific service, and even had hands laid on her, but she was not given the same ministry as the male deacon. There is no apparent, valid reason not to ordain or recognize the female deacon.

I am aware that many traditionalists will argue that female deacons are not ordained because they are not properly tested/ evaluated. There is no valid reason why the female deacon should not be tested/evaluated, just as the male deacon is. In fact, as the female deacon is set apart to perform specific services for God, she is required to have the same knowledge as the male deacon. Therefore, the deaconess MUST be properly tested/evaluated to ensure her readiness.[38] When her readiness is confirmed, she should be properly ordained, and recognized as so. In this area, please don't confuse a deacon's wife with a deaconess. A deacon's wife may not necessarily be a deaconess; a deaconess does not have to be a deacon's wife.[39] The emphasis here is on the female person that meets the prerequisites and qualifications, and has the calling and desire to serve in this ministry. This person has the God-given right to serve and must be given the opportunity to serve within her call and/or ministry, just as any male deacon.

We must not continue to place value on individuals based solely on gender? Today, it appears that the word "woman" is still just another term for the old biblical word "gentile." Man is a Jew (one of the chosen and privileged), and woman is a gentile (an outsider/invalid). Are women less saved than men? Is it a matter of spirituality? Are women limited to a level of spirituality below that of men? **God is a spirit, and how spiritual one is, or can become, depends upon how much control one yields to the Holy Spirit, not to gender.**[40] The Holy Spirit is the gift of God, given to all that accept Jesus Christ as their personal Lord and Savior. Salvation and spirituality come from God and are available to all through Jesus Christ; no person has an advantage or privilege over another. Furthermore, Matthew 27:51 tells us, **"And Behold, The Veil Of The Temple Was Rent In Twain From Top To Bottom"** (*emphasis added*). The veil in the temple represented divisions (mankind from mankind and mankind from God). The veil could not be penetrated except by the High Priest, on the Day of Atonement. The Spirit of God dwelt behind the veil. Up to that time, there was an eclipse between God and man. But, in the death of Jesus, the eclipse was removed and the way to the presence of God, once barred from all, was opened to all. The life and death of Jesus show us what God is like/about and removed forever the veil and divisions that separated us from his love and presence.

Let's not make the same mistake the Old Testament Jews made. Because God gave the Jews His word first, they thought they had a monopoly on Him; however, they had no more value or priority than others had with Him.[41] God chose not to give the word to the entire world at the same time. In the truest sense, it only made them responsible for sharing the word with others.

Whatever God gives you He wants you to bless others by sharing. God made man first and gave him dominion, but that didn't
give him a monopoly on God, nor was man given more value or
priority over woman, in terms of his relationship with God. God
only gave man responsibility first. The Jews receiving the word
first (or God making man first) has nothing to do with the Jews
or man, but rather, everything to do with God.[42] God reserves the
right to give responsibility to anything or anybody He chooses.
God is unlimited in what he can do or use to fulfill His will. He
is not "boxed in," or limited, by nature or mankind. All that
exists is available to Him to use when and how He pleases. So
let's stop trying to "box in" (limit) God.

As we look at the condition of our families today, we see
more and more of them being "headed" by females. Needless to
say, there are many needs/aspects about women that men just
don't understand. There are many needs that can only be properly handled by the female deacon. Today's church must have
the deaconess doing more than just wearing white and sitting on
the front row, waiting for another annual day. The female deacon, like the male deacon, must be busy meeting people's needs.

Many traditionalists will take a stand against this point,
based on Old Testament practices. Please keep in mind, however, that many of those practices went away with Jesus' coming.
In layman's terms, Jesus came because his people's needs
weren't being met. Oftentimes it was due to the traditionalists.
If those traditions weren't good then, what makes one believe
they are now? People's needs have changed; when will the traditions? Furthermore, the Bible makes it very clear that God is
not limited, and He can and will use anything or anybody to get
his will accomplished. There are many examples in the
Scriptures of God's use of women. Prophetesses and deaconesses are excellent examples. Acts 10:34-35, Romans 2:11 and

Galatians 3:28 inform us that in Christ there are no males or females, and that God is no respecter of persons--thank God.

I don't mean to stress this point over tradition, lessening the value and service of women in God's vineyard, but some traditions don't seem logical, thus overriding spiritual purpose. For example, women cannot serve the elements of communion, yet they prepare them. Are there differences in the elements of communion when they are prepared? When they are served? Aren't they the same elements? Secondly, the elements are symbolic of Jesus' suffering. Mary, the mother of Jesus, carried and handled the Messiah himself. Surely if God used a woman to bring the Messiah into the world, we can use women in the process of remembering him symbolically. Are our actions saying that women are less spiritual or less valuable to God?[43]

Let's stop majoring on minors and start majoring on the majors. Most of the issues we spend time and effort arguing about in the church don't contribute to salvation or the needs of the people. We spend valuable time arguing over mundane issues while the greater matters go unnoticed. If a matter doesn't pertain to salvation and/or meeting the needs of the people, then it's not worth being hung up on. Too many deacons think they can run a church at a board meeting, by being hung up over issues that really don't matter. This is only a tactic to sidetrack the man of God from prayer and study of the word.

Now, let's discuss the individual qualifications of the deacon, given by Luke and Paul in the Books of Acts and Timothy, respectively. In Acts 6:3 the disciples were instructed to look out among themselves to find certain types of men to serve in this most critical position. A better word for "look" is "seek," which carries the idea of putting forth effort to search, examine, inquire, investigate, pry and question. The seven that were chosen had to have the witness of others. Their fellow disciples had to observe their character and moral attributes prior to the selection process. Note that the Apostles did not give the qualifications and then ask for volunteers. It's not enough for one to have a good opinion of oneself--others must have the same opinion. Traditionally, no word was accepted as true without at least two witnesses. There was evidence that the first men chosen manifested a depth of judiciousness to deal with that old matter of discrimination. Today's deacon must have this quality in order to properly serve in the church.

An Honest Report

A deacon must have, first of all, an <u>Honest Report</u>. His background must be impeccably clear. Doing the Lord's work is "serious business." If a man has a shaky background, is apt to steal or easily swayed, he might give in to the temptations of the past. That would only result in shame. Not only would he be affected by such misbehavior, but the church would be tainted as well. A man's good reputation will always outlast his deeds and fortune. This kind of man must follow instructions to the letter because too often churches are overly confident about the people whom they put in office, even though they have no background for service. No one should be able to say aught against a deacon's personal life, at work, home or church.

Today's deacons must be men and women that are upright, fair, just, faithful, free from fraud, and have unadulterated/ unquestionable honesty and a good reputation in the church and community alike. The people whom the deacon serves should have the highest level of confidence in him. It is a tragic thing for a church to have a deacon whose honesty and trust are in question. Such a person should not be in the position of deacon. The duties of the deacon call for the highest level of confidence. As a leader, and as a servant of the people, the deacon must have the trust of the pastor, church and community alike.[44]

Full of the Holy Spirit

It is not at all hard to find a man whose moral life is without guile. It is not hard to find a man liked by almost everybody in the church. But to ask for a man who has a good report--and is spirit-filled--is asking a great deal. The Apostles did not just want good men, they wanted men with boldness to speak as the spirit led them. They needed men with zeal to go forward and pioneer developments that were undernourished. This is exhibited in the strong preaching of Stephen and Phillip. The Apostles knew that a spirit-filled man would be apt to pray and seek the Lord's guidance. A man of the spirit could be counseled if he was wrong and accept that consultation in a spirit and attitude of meekness. A man that is inhabited by the spirit shines, not because he is exalted, but because the Spirit glows through his humility. It was quite natural for the Apostles to want spiritual men to direct the business matters. Whenever trouble approached and threatened to create chaos and havoc, these men would allow the Holy Spirit to work and bring forth correction and beauty. The pastors of today need spiritually minded persons to stand with them, especially in the time of crises and criticism.

The word "full" carries the idea of being covered in every part, thoroughly permeated with, complete and lacking nothing. It represents whole-heartedness, total sincerity, and complete dedication and commitment. **Being full of the Holy Spirit does not mean how much of the Holy Spirit one possesses, but rather how much of one does the Holy Spirit possess.** One must yield himself to the control of the Holy Spirit. Only God knows what is right, in terms of his people's needs; and the Holy

Spirit is the source for the information. No one can adequately serve God's people without being led by the Holy Spirit. Being controlled by, or having a personal dedication to the directives of, the Holy Spirit is the only way to an overall spiritual outlook. Deacons must be full of the Holy Spirit in order to discern matters that they are confronted with. The pastor should not be bothered with petty issues.

Wisdom

One must understand that wisdom does not come overnight.[45] Wisdom usually develops out of time, experience and maturity. Improper use of knowledge produces hasty, spur-of-the-moment decisions. Wisdom is more than knowledge. It involves the knowledge of God and the intricacies of the human heart.[46] It is the right application of knowledge in moral and spiritual matters, when resolving baffling situations and in dealing with the complexities of human relationships. Knowledge is gained by study, but when the Spirit fills a man, God imparts the wisdom to use and apply that knowledge correctly.

The New Testament makes the uncontested point that God's paramount concern is with the moral and spiritual character of those who lead and care for His people. The deacon must be one who is known and respected by the congregation. The words respectable and honorable should convey the meaning of persons whose moral and spiritual characters evoke esteem from others. Stephen, one of the seven described in Acts 6, was honorable and respected by all.[47] Paul required deacons to be worthy of respect. This corresponds with the Apostles' qualification for them in Acts 6:3, that the deacon be "of good reputation." Of good reputation means that the seven had to be men whose good character and skills were known and well spoken of. Their character had to be certified by their public testimony.

Full of wisdom means wise in the sense that one has developed the skill of correctly applying knowledge in a given situation. Individuals act and choose wisely when they are led wisely. Based on today's standard, this does not necessarily mean that the deacon has to be a learned individual. Learned individuals are not always wise individuals. One should be an individual of good judgment--knowing the appropriate thing to do in a given situation. Note what James 1:5 says: "IF ANY OF YOU LACK WISDOM, LET HIM ASK OF GOD, THAT GIVETH TO ALL MEN LIBERALLY" (*emphasis added*). Being full of the Holy Spirit and full of wisdom are inseparable. The Holy Spirit brings/gives the information, while wisdom instructs the use of the information to reach the appropriate outcome. Having knowledge is not enough--one must also have the wisdom to apply it appropriately. Knowledge without wisdom is like a train running on a track without an engineer--out of control.

Paul's first letter to Timothy focuses on his charge to Timothy. Paul appeals to him to maintain the things that he had been entrusted with, which included certain established standards in the Christian Church. Two of the standards were the qualifications of the bishops and deacons, the two biblical church officers. The following are the qualifications of the deacon, given by Paul in Chapter 3 of 1 Timothy.[48]

Grave

Grave is defined as being serious about life; having a certain dignity; a consciousness of human worth and divine privilege; a right relationship with God; respect for others; having the quality of venerability; being dignified in one's appearance and manner; having high ideals and practicing them in contact with others; enjoying life without indulging in matters that will lower one's character. This individual's word carries weight with man and God.[49]

Not Double Tongued

Those who will do the work of the Christian Church must be unwavering in certain matters. They must go from house to house and deal with those who need help. They must be honest and straightforward. Again and again, one could be tempted to evade issues by operating in hypocrisy and using smooth, beguiling speech. There are, however, some principles that must not be compromised. They must have the truth in their heart and mind, speaking to all only that which they feel and believe to be right, and not straddle the fence by saying one thing to one person and the opposite to another. They must not intentionally say anything that could be misinterpreted or have a double meaning. They must avoid situations that will cause them to be untrue to themselves.

Not Given to Much Wine

Many brethren have taken a great deal of comfort from the appearance that while the pastor is not to use wine, the deacon is simply not to use much wine. They would interpret that as long as one does not drink alcohol, as some say, in excess, it is permissible. There is no real ground for believing that a double standard is created in the Scriptures. A deacon has a responsibility towards God in the matter of alcoholic drink. A fair examination of the Bible indicates that the one who will be faithful to his vow (that which officially sets one apart as an officer/servant of the church) must leave intoxicating drink out of his life. Numbers 6:1-4 sets the standard for anyone that makes a vow. It tells us that when either a man or a woman shall separate (vow) themselves unto the Lord,

...HE SHALL SEPARATE HIMSELF FROM WINE AND STRONG DRINK, AND SHALL DRINK NO VINEGAR OF WINE, OR VINEGAR OF STRONG DRINK, NEITHER SHALL HE DRINK ANY LIQUOR OF GRAPES, NOR EAT MOIST GRAPES, OR DRIED. (*Emphasis added.*)

Also, John the Baptist was an example of this standard, in Luke 1:15: "For he shall be great in the sight of the Lord, and shall neither drink wine nor strong drink."

Many use 1 Timothy 5:23 to justify their use of alcoholic drink as a beverage. Paul did not suggest that it was okay for Timothy to use wine in this fashion. Paul directed Timothy to no longer drink the water; and he encouraged him to take a little wine for his stomach's sake, or for frequent illnesses. The water was bad and oftentimes caused illnesses. The wine was more pure than the drinking water. Even today many of the medicines we take contain a high percentage of alcohol. The problem we encounter with alcohol today is the way it's used as a beverage.

Furthermore, this qualification carries the idea of one always being at his level best--refraining from anything that will intoxicate, excite or stupefy him to the point where his physical and/or mental control is diminished. If a deacon is to serve and lead by example, he must (1) be temperate in his living, (2) be a steward of good influence and (3) do all things for the glory of God. Ask yourself this simple question: "Does God get glory out of what I'm doing?"

Not Greedy of Filthy Lucre

Deacons must have the right attitude toward material possessions and not be eager to exploit others for their own gain or profit. They must be honest and show the utmost level of integrity in their dealings with others. To not be greedy of filthy lucre means that one does not have an insatiable love of money. In fact, 1 Timothy 6:10 is one of the most misquoted Scriptures in the Bible. The Scripture does not say that "money" is the root of all evil; it says that "the love of money" is the root of all evil. Money, in itself, is neither good nor bad; but the love for it may lead to evil. With it one may selfishly serve his own desires; with it one may answer the cry of his neighbor's need. Money is a great responsibility, and it can cause potential evil if used inappropriately. It is powerful, and it can be used for good and for evil. What, then, are the special dangers involved in loving money?

The desire for money can ultimately lead to an insatiable thirst. There is an old Roman proverbial saying: *Wealth is like seawater, so far from quenching a man's thirst it intensifies it.* The more one gets, the more one wants, and the more selfish one becomes. The love of money may easily lead one to do wrong and, in the end, result in remorse and mental and physical pain. One may drive his body in his passion to get that which ruins his health. One may discover, oftentimes too late, the possible damage his desire has done to others and become burdened with remorse.[50]

If one is driven by the desire for wealth, it is nothing to him that someone has to lose in order that he may gain. The desire for wealth can cause selfishness, and others merely become means or obstacles in the path to self-enrichment. Wealth is found on an illusion: the desire for security. But wealth cannot buy security. It cannot buy health or real love. It cannot preserve from sorrow and keep one from death. Security founded on material things is foredoomed to failure.[51] Although the desire for wealth is based on security, it ends in nothing but anxiety. The more one has to keep, the more one has to lose. And the tendency for him to be haunted by the risk of loss increases.

To seek to be independent and to prudently provide for the future is a Christian duty, but to overindulge or make the love of money the driving force can never be anything other than the most perilous of sins. Money has its value and is needed to live in today's society, but it must be kept in its proper perspective in the overall scheme of life.

From a broader perspective, this biblical qualification is a warning against covetousness--the eager, driving desire to possess that which belongs to another. This is a condition of the heart which oftentimes results in the taking of things that rightfully belong to another. Needless to say, this is in no way limited to money, but rather can be anything (reference: the "Ten Commandments" in the twentieth Chapter of Exodus). Covetousness will ruin any Christian's life. Life is truly about building relationships, and covetousness will truly destroy relationships. To help prevent the above from occurring, trust God to be true to his word. Matthew 6:33 says, "BUT SEEK YE FIRST THE KINGDOM OF GOD, AND HIS RIGHTEOUSNESS; AND ALL THESE THINGS SHALL BE ADDED UNTO YOU" (*emphasis added*). If we are obedient Christians, God will take care of all the necessities in our lives, including security.

Holding the Mystery of Faith with a Good Conscience

The mystery of faith means the revelation of the Gospel of Christ. When Paul says "the faith," he is not speaking of the abstract quality of faith, but of the doctrines and teachings of the faith. He speaks of it as a "mystery" because these doctrines were not revealed in the Old Testament, but are now revealed in the New Testament through Jesus Christ. The spiritual qualifications that the Bible lays down for the church and its officers must hold good if the church is to represent our Lord and Savior, Jesus Christ. They must be faithful and obedient to His teachings, which are the eternal purpose of God.[52]

"In a pure conscience" carries the same idea as 1 Timothy 4:2--that is, having a conscience that has not been seared with a hot iron. Here, Paul takes the time to share the Ephesus situation to make his point clear. False teachers had entered into the church at Ephesus. Many believed that evil spirits haunted the air and were out to ruin men. These spirits came from demons and manifested themselves through men who practiced smooth hypocrisy and whose consciences had been branded by Satan. In certain instances, owners branded their slaves with marks, identifying them as their property. It is sad to say that many deacons operate as though they have the brand of Satan. They are out to destroy the pastor, church and ministry, in the name of the Lord. This is not indicative of faithful deacons that really have the church at heart. Those false teachers bear upon their consciences the very brand of Satan. They are marked as his property and do his will.

God is always searching for individuals who will be his instruments in the world, but the terrible fact is, is that the forces of evil are also looking for individuals to use. Individuals may accept either the services of God or the services of the devil. The person that holds the mystery of faith in a pure conscience is the person that (1) makes Jesus his Lord and Master, and remains faithful (will not sell out) in spite of situations and/or circumstances and (2) knows God's truths and stands on His Word.

Proved

A person should not be allowed (or forced) to become a deacon a month after he has joined the church. He has not proven that he is the type of person that the Scriptures describe. This statement may sound "off the wall," but it serves well in making this point. Individuals with the wrong qualifications, and for the wrong reasons, are selected as deacons--not that their qualifications are *morally* wrong. In fact, they may have qualifications that are very much needed, and would be a real plus in today's society, but they are not part of the Scriptural basis for choosing deacons. Scripture does not support the selection of individuals solely because they are educated, intellectual, political, financially secure, skillful in business, etc. Scripture only describes spiritual and/or godly qualifications. Again, these must be evident in the life of the individual that will serve in this capacity. Paul advises a trial period for deacon candidates. Although no formal test is implied, evidence must be gathered. This same implication appears in 1 Timothy 3:6 with regard to Paul's instruction that a pastor must not be a recent convert. If, after a specified trial period, the candidate is found faithful at carrying out his responsibilities, let him be formally ordained as a deacon.

(A SIDE NOTE: To prove anything, a concentrated effort must be made by someone to look, search, investigate or at least question qualifications.)

Questions such as the ones listed below should be asked and answered, according to the standards required by God, before one is made a deacon.

1. What is known about the individual being considered (other than what is obvious on Sundays)?

2. How long has the individual been a member of God's kingdom (saved)?

3. How long has the individual been a faithful member of the church?

4. What kind of service has the individual rendered in the church?

5. What is it about the individual's life that indicates he is NOW ready for this most critical service?

Blameless

This is a support qualification for *"Proved."* During a deacon's trial period, there must be evidence of this spiritual qualifications and service rendered. But just as importantly, there must not be any evidence of "corruption." Whereas "sin" is missing the mark, "corruption" is purposely not trying to hit the target. There is a major difference in willfully or intentionally doing wrong versus trying to do as God would have us to do but erring in the process. Please don't confuse blameless with sinless. Blameless does not mean an individual is perfect (without sin or fault). A requirement of perfection would eliminate us all; people are not perfect, in the literal sense. Blameless does mean that no charge of intentional wrongdoing has been brought against one. In essence, one is trying to live in the manner in which God would have him to live. God looks at our hearts, not just our actions. A more in-depth meaning is that one has accepted Jesus Christ as his personal Savior and Lord--accepting Jesus' blood payment, on the cross, for his sins. Therefore, one will no longer be blamed or held responsible for sin, as he stands before God; for Jesus took upon himself the blame and charges for sin.

Husband of One Wife

This is one of the most controversial and abused qualifications of a deacon. We have taken the phrase "husband of only one wife" to mean several things. The phrase "husbands of only one wife" and its related phrase, "the wife of one man," occur four times in the New Testament in the context of qualifications for either overseers, deacons or widows. This phrase apparently expresses an exemplary Christian marital relationship: a husband-and-wife relationship that is above reproach. This type of relationship is spoken of four times in Scriptures:

- An overseer, then, must be above reproach, the husband of one wife, temperate, prudent, respectable, hospitable, able to teach ... (1 Timothy 3:2)

- Let deacons be husbands of only one wife, and good managers of their children and their own households. (1 Timothy 3:12)

- Let a widow be put on the list only if she is not less than sixty years old, having been the wife of one. (1 Timothy 5:9)

- ...if any man be above reproach, the husband of one wife, having children who believe, not accused of dissipation or rebellion. (Titus 1:6)

There are many interpretations of the Scriptures that are traditional rather than biblical. It's not uncommon for people to say that deacons (and overseers) must be married because Scripture says they must be the "husbands of only one wife." If Paul requires them to be married, however, he flatly contradicts what he teaches in 1 Corinthians 7 about the distinct advantages of singleness in serving the Lord. He boldly encourages singleness because it disqualifies an aspiring overseer or deacon. Paul didn't write, however, "Deacons must be men who have wives." He says that they must be *one-wife men*, which is quite a different point. Singleness does not disqualify a deacon.The fact is most men are married and have children. Scripture requires that these men have their homes in order and that their marital relationships exemplify what Christian marriage should be. These qualifications don't apply to deacons who are single.

The local church is perfectly designed to protect, support and teach each Christian family. Therefore, Christian families need the local church. They need sound biblical teaching. They need to be shown God's wonderful design for the Christian home. They need to see good models of fatherhood and motherhood. They need to be under the disciplinary authority of the church. (Matthew 18:17-20; 1 Corinthians 5; 2 Thessalonians 3:6-15; Titus 3:10)

A local church that is alive and functioning properly can help numerous families. Shepherds and deacons are chief among those who model God's design for the Christian home and provide sound teaching on Christian family life. This is one reason why God demands that their homes and marriages be in order.

A crucial step in Satan's strategy to destroy God's people is to destroy the marriages and families of those who lead the church. If he defiles the shepherds, the sheep will follow their sinful ways--or be scattered. To protect the local church, God has placed specific marital and family qualifications for elders and deacons. Therefore, the church must insist that its leaders meet these qualifications while (and before) they serve. If not, the local church will sink into the toxic wasteland of the world's marital and family values.

In marriage, child-rearing and general home management,

deacons and elders must model God's design: they must have faithful, monogamous marriages, and loving, disciplined Christian households. In these fundamental areas of Christian life, deacons must be above reproach. They must be "husbands of only one wife" and "good managers of their children and their own households."

Another phrase in the church is, "Deacons must be married only once." Some prominent scholars and biblical commentators believe that this phrase means "married only once" and that deacons cannot remarry. Paul, they believe, prohibits remarriage for any reason, even remarriage following the death of a spouse. Thus a widower who remarried could not become a deacon; and if a deacon's wife died, he could not remain a deacon if he remarries. This interpretation is plainly at odds with the rest of the Bible's teaching on the sanctity of marriage. Nowhere else in the New Testament is there the slightest trace of any ordinance against second marriages.

By itself, the phrase "husbands of only one wife" doesn't indicate whether each husband is to have one wife in an entire lifetime or one wife at a time. This phrase, therefore, must be interpreted in the larger context of Paul's overall teaching on marriage and must never be allowed to contradict God's clear, general teaching on marriage. It is highly questionable that this phrase is meant to disqualify remarried widowers. Therefore, a remarried widower could still qualify to be called a "one-wife man." Some apply this phrase only to remarriage after a divorce, not the death of a spouse.

Among Jews, Romans and Greeks it was easy to divorce and remarry. In the case of remarriage after a divorce, unlike the death of a spouse, two or three living women could have been married to the same man. Some have termed this successive polygamy. They believe Paul prohibits a remarried divorcee from office because his ex-wife (or ex-wives) creates for the deacon, and the congregation, potentially offensive, embarrassing or vulnerable situations. However, if Paul specifically intended to prohibit divorced and remarried men from holding office, he would have precisely said so. It is necessary that we take a fresh look at this qualification by referring to what our Lord and Teacher, Jesus Christ, best explained God's design for marriage to be.

> Have you not read, that He who created them from the beginning made them male and female, and said, "For this cause a man shall leave his father and mother, and shall cleave to his wife; and the two shall become one flesh"? Consequently they *are no longer two, but one flesh. What therefore God has joined together, let no man separate.*
> (Matthew 19:4b-6, *Emphasis added*)

We must consider this: "What kind of relationship does the candidate for office in the local church have with his wife and other women?" Scripture answers that the candidate be a "one-wife" or "one-woman" man. A "one-woman" man has an exclusive relationship with one woman.

The phrase "husbands of only one wife" naturally raises agonizing questions. For example, what about sexual and marital sins committed before a person's conversion to Christ? What about people who have legally divorced and remarried (assuming the local church allows for such)? What about the forgiveness and restoration of a fallen spiritual leader? These and many more questions must be answered from the whole of the Scripture's teachings on divorce and remarriage, forgiveness, grace, restoration, leadership example and qualification.

All deviations from God's marital standards confuse and perplex us. They raise painfully controversial questions. Sin always confuses, distorts and divides; so there will always be diverse opinions on questions such as the previous ones. This in no way, however, diminishes the local church's obligation to face these issues and make wise, scripturally sound decisions. In all of these issues and heartbreaking situations, the honor of Jesus' name, faithfulness to His word, and prayer are the Supreme guidelines.

Ruler of His Own House

A person must have the love and respect of his family or household. This is gained by first demonstrating love and respect. One must lead by example, thus setting the "tone" and establishing the right atmosphere for a healthy, functional family. Power and authority need not be exerted over family members. Normally, one does not have to deal harshly or be domineering in order to get desired results--assuming those results are within God's will, and will give God His glory and honor. One can get results by leading, guiding and directing, in love. Clear and precise objectives, goals, expectations, guidelines and, even, rules (hopefully a select few) must be shared. My mother referred to the rules governing her home as "house rules." The rules remained the same no matter who was in the house. More often than not, everyone knew and obeyed the house rules; this helped to create a peaceful household.

Naturally, family members know who is in charge and will usually remain respectful if they are taught discipline and self-control. People are not animals with instincts that direct them to do the appropriate thing at the appropriate time. Through instinct, the trout swims upstream for the mating season. Without thought or planning, the trout naturally goes to the right place at the right time, and does the right thing; whereas, people must be taught. In managing one's own house well, people must be instructed on what to do, and be shown through example. This builds credibility and respect with the family. The person who tells his household what to do but does differently himself, will not be successful at leading his family. Behaviors and expectations must be consistent for all.

When one is successfully managing his own house, he is, then, more prepared to do what is necessary for God's house (the church). This carries the idea of service. When one learns how to serve his own, then and only then is he really prepared to serve others. There are three reasons why it is critical to learn to serve one's own before attempting to serve others. **First**, one must know the appropriate things to do at the appropriate time--there's no teacher like experience. **Second**, one cannot concentrate on and remain consistent at serving others if he is constantly being called on to put out fires and solve problems within his own household. In order to be available to serve others, one must have his house in order. **Third**, one must serve with tender care and love, as Jesus did.

The Deacon and His Calling

The origin and work of the deacon is rooted in at least five theological suppositions. These suppositions convey Christ's concern for all men; the recognition of man's limitations; man's inability to meet his needs (alone); and the imperfection of the visible, organized church structure (including the strengths and weaknesses of men) to do its work and meet the needs of the members at all times. The eternal cry of the needy--when neglected or discriminated against by those in authority or when certain basic human needs are not met--and an organized plan to strengthen the church to spread its responsibilities among more of the members and to establish a division of labor as a specific task to certain individuals, are all theological suppositions.

A person does not become a deacon just for the honor. The deacon is set apart to serve. He is committed to serve God and his fellowman. **The office of deacon is not one of authority, but one of service.** The original purpose for the establishment of deacon service was to preserve the spiritual fellowship of the church.

The deacon's function is that of an assistant to the pastor. He is chosen by the church at the suggestion of the pastor, to do a threefold task as the need occurs. He is to responsibly serve the needs of church members and be ready, prepared and available for opportunities to serve Christ, throughout the church. He is also to serve as an assistant with responsibilities and in cooperation with the pastor of the church.

The Deacon's Relationship to the Church

The deacon and pastor comprise a team that should be most intimately connected and thoroughly cooperative in the work of the Lord and in the service of the church. The necessary characteristics of a man who is selected to serve as a deacon are the following:

(1) He must be willing to be all that God wants him to be.

(2) He must be willing to do all the church wants him to do.

(3) He must have earned the right to be respected as a thorough going Christian.

(4) He must and be aware of what he can

become as a result of spiritual growth through prayer, study and the grace of God--he must never be satisfied with himself as he is.

(5) He must know God and the members of the church firsthand.

The Deacon--Partner with His Pastor

When one is named a deacon of the church, he becomes a partner in service with his pastor. All persons need emotional support from others. The pastor has a right to expect support from all the members--deacons included. And the people should expect support from the deacons, the pastor and others in the fellowship. Pastors and deacons must adopt the team concept: "For we are laborers together with God" (1 Corinthians 3:10).

In Christ's Church, there should be no empire builders-- there are no solo performers. The forward motion the church experiences when it accomplishes the purposes of Christ will either be slowed or stopped if the pastor and deacons do not operate as a team.

Pastors and Deacons Share Similar Qualifications

Man does not set the leader's qualifications. God gave divine insight to the Apostle Paul as he set forth qualities of spiritual life that both pastors and deacons are to possess. Grave danger can result if the church lowers the qualifications of either of these Christian leaders. 1 Timothy 3 speaks of the kind of persons both leaders are to be: Spiritual men on a spiritual mission. Each should be in the process of becoming.

The Differences in the Pastor's and Deacon's Leadership Roles

The church calls the pastor to be a generalist leader. In his leadership role, the pastor serves as a player-coach-enabler. He develops people. As generalist leader he leads the church to determine its spiritual mission.

Deacons are exemplary leaders. They serve as models for fellow Christians to follow. As exemplary leaders, deacons often serve behind the scenes--out of the spotlight or central focus of activities. Some guidelines for deacons to follow will be contingent upon understanding the pastor and his work. Being a pastor is like many other tasks in life; and yet it is unlike anything else in the world. It is about being loved and unloved, wanted and unwanted, understood and misunderstood. At times it is heaven; at other times it is hell. The pastor needs friends. He needs people who will keep his confidences and share with him during moments of loneliness. Deacons and other laity must understand the pastor and his work.

Deacons should pray for the pastor. Laity must lift up the pastor in daily prayers (public and private)--thanking God for him and his ministry--and stop by his office and join him in prayer, as well. They will be affirmed as they affirm, support and fellowship with the pastor. When deacons take the leadership in sponsoring the Pastor's Appreciation Day, they are saying, "Pastor, we love you." Because the deacon is the pastor's moral and spiritual helper in service to the people, he should be supportive of his pastor. The partnership or team concept means that laity and clergy can depend on each other. They must practice being open, honest and loving in all relationships. The deacons are expected to be men of integrity, consecration and wisdom. They should be knowledgeable of their duties and in full sympathy with the policies of their leaders.

The Deacon's Ministry

The deacon seeks not his own will, but to know and do the will of Christ and the church he serves. The deacons help the pastor by praying with and for him, encouraging him, defending him when he is criticized unfairly, being frank with him when it is thought that he is mistaken, and by being his moral and spiritual helper in service to the people.

The deacons help the church by attending the services; participating in the work of the church; supporting the financial program of the church; encouraging indifferent members and praising the faithful ones; discouraging envy, jealousy, backbiting and strife; refraining from gossip, and insisting that the truth be told about all matters; and guarding confidences.

The Deacon Translates His Qualifications into Service

God, in His Divine wisdom, set the qualifications (listed below) for a deacon high because the work of the deacon is spiritual in nature.

A MAN OF HONEST REPORT (Acts 6:13)--good reputation among those in the church as well as those outside the church.

FULL OF THE HOLY SPIRIT (Acts 6:3)--bigness of character in spiritual outlook and personal dedication.

FULL OF WISDOM (Acts 6:5)--an ability to discern right or wrong and to stand for personal convictions.

FULL OF FAITH (Acts 6:5)--like Stephen; a deacon's faith requires him to risk himself and his possessions.

GRAVE (1 Timothy 3:8)--possesses Christian purpose and has great reverence for spiritual matters; his word carries weight.

NOT DOUBLE-TONGUED (1 Timothy 3:8)--temperate in living, steward of good influence, does all to the glory of God.

NOT GIVEN TO MUCH WINE (1 Timothy 3:8)--dependable and honest in relating to all persons publicly and privately.

NOT GREEDY OF FILTHY LUCRE (1 Timothy 3:8)--right attitude toward material possessions, never exploiting others for personal own gain.

A HOLDER OF THE FAITH (1 Timothy 3:9)--gives strength to the church fellowship and possesses spiritual integrity beyond reproach.

TESTED AND PROVEN (1 Timothy 3:10)--demonstrates his commitment to the ministry before being elected to serve as a deacon.

BLAMELESS (1 Timothy 3:10)--person against whom no charge of wrongdoing can be brought with success.

CHRISTIAN FAMILY LIFE (1 Timothy 3:11-12)--person whose family is well cared for, whose family relationships are healthy and growing.

HUSBAND OF ONE WIFE (1 Timothy 3:12)--model of faithful devotion to one spouse, committed to the sanctity of the marriage bond.

RULES HIS CHILDREN AND HIS OWN HOUSE WELL (1 Timothy 3:12)--loved and respected by all family members, caring for them as Jesus cared for others.

BOLD IN FAITH (1 Timothy 3:13)--holds firmly to what he believes, taking every opportunity for ministry.

The prayer of the deacon should well be the same as St. Augustine's, who once prayed, *"O Lord, grant that I may do thy will as if it were my will; so that I mayest do my will as if it were thy will."*[53]

Deacons Should Discover, Develop and Nurture Their Spiritual Gifts

God has given special gifts. Deacons are unlike other leaders. They are created like a distinctive snowflake or a fingerprint. Deacons have been given special talents. Every deacon should discover, develop and nurture his spiritual gifts.

CHAPTER THREE

UNDERSTANDING THE ROLE & RESPONSIBILITIES OF THE PASTOR

Who is the Pastor?

The main obstacle in the inability of deacons to minister to their pastor is they do not understand his role and responsibilities. Deacons many times do not have their vision of God's kingdom evaluated beyond the laity (laos). They often think too much like laity, as opposed to spiritual leaders.[54] Thus their own vision of who the pastor is, is normally shaped by tradition--or by the history of their relationship with the pastor prior to being called out as a leader. There are two traditional concepts that must be overcome: The **first** is that the pastor is someone who is only interested in money. Deacons must recognize that church money does not belong to a church officer or to an official church group. It is first the Lord's and then the congregations--to distribute under the leadership of the Holy Spirit. It is indeed easy for young men and women to get a sense of proprietorship about money. However, the tithe brought to the church ceases to belong to the one who brings it.

The **second** traditional concept is that the pastor is someone who is to preach only, and anything he does outside of preaching is non-spiritual. This type of attitude fosters contention, causing both sides to closely watch each other. However, the Biblical model of who the pastor is, is a shepherd that **pursues**, **protects** and **provides** for the sheep. Therefore, it becomes vitally important for deacons to minister to their pastor in order to reduce the stress and spiritual strain often placed upon him.

The relationship between a pastor and deacon should be guided by the Holy Spirit. The deacon must view the preacher in the light of New Testament teaching, recognizing that God has created his office in order to make the pastor's ministry more effective. This starts by first knowing that he is a person as well as a pastor. By knowing who the pastor is, deacons can become aware of his strengths and weaknesses. In return, they should attempt to help the pastor maintain his strong areas and improve in the weak. Strengths can be maintained if deacons pray for their pastor and make sure that he has the private time he needs to pray and seek God. Weaknesses must not be exposed; rather, the deacons should encourage the pastor to get help in areas where help is needed, and commit themselves to providing the resources the pastor needs in order to get the necessary help. Also, the deacons should pray that he overcomes his weaknesses and that they, as leaders, may be used of God to minister to the pastor and people. Thus, overcoming weaknesses becomes a witness to God's power.

The pastor should provide a spiritual model regarding the relationship between pastor and deacon (Exodus 18:13-22). The story of Jethro and Moses reflects this need. Utilizing spiritual models makes it easier for the people to allow deacons to counsel them in matters, thus freeing the pastor's time. The seven (in

Acts 6) were chosen that they might free the Apostles for prayer and ministry of the word. Pastors must be set free--not so much **"free from"** as **"free to do the work"** of the ministry. The text in Exodus 18:13-22 reflects Jethro's spiritual sensitivity and overall concern for the welfare of Moses, who, at the time, was being overworked. By providing a spiritual model, the pastor is able to open up to the deacons regarding ministries as well as personal concerns, without fear of backlash. A spiritual model will always seek to minister, not condemn or tear down. These sensitivities toward the things of God are a must if there is to be absolute trust between pastor and deacon. The spiritual model includes praying for the pastor and his family without ceasing; oneness; trust; and the belief that if the pastor is truly sent by God, then as deacons they are the stewards of God's gift to the church. (May I never abuse it.)

Deacons should be sensitive to the material needs of the pastor, such as food, clothing, shelter, transportation and additional training. By ensuring that these needs are met, the pastor is able to more freely minister to the congregation. In Philippians 4:15-18, Paul speaks of how he did not have to ask the church at Philippi for financial help. They were aware of his situation and acted upon it. Paul never mentioned his condition of need; they were moved by the spirit only as they made themselves sensitive to his needs. Deacons should not turn the pastor into a beggar by causing him to ask for what he needs. Ask God to give you direction, and open yourself up to being used by God to meet needs. "I will set up shepherds over them who will care for them and they shall fear no more, nor be dismayed, neither shall they be lacking, saith the Lord" (Jeremiah 23:4).

Role and Responsibility of the Pastor

The pastor is the spiritual and administrative head of the church. As spiritual leader, he is to teach and preach the Gospel and provide leadership, as God directs him, in developing the various ministries. The pastor's role and responsibility can be clearly defined by the example Jesus set in Matthew 4:23, and also by the seven shepherd models given by Dr. Benjamin S. Baker in his book *Shepherding the Sheep*.

A. The Four Pastoral Models--Matthew 4:23

- Preach
- Teach
- Heal
- Pray

B. The Seven Shepherd Models

1. Shepherd

The pastor is the shepherd of the flock. He has been called by God to be an earthly undershepherd, with the responsibility of feeding, leading and training the sheep in the way the Lord has ordained for his people to follow. The pastor, as a shepherd, needs to be mindful that he is both accountable and responsible to Jesus Christ, the Good Shepherd, for their care and handling, and their protection and provisions.[55]

2. Overseer--(Acts 20:28)

The pastor-overseer is to oversee the flock of God. The first responsibility of this pastoral model is for the pastor to take heed unto himself. He must know who he is and whose he is. His identity must be God-given and not people defined. He **must** see himself as pastor. His task is to feed, care for, lead and train the flock of God in the lifestyle the Lord has ordained for his people to follow.[56]

3. Supervisor--(Matthew 10:1-8)

The pastor-supervisor is to help the members feel the dignity of given tasks and develop their personal initiative, and pledge his encouragement and support. The tools, gifts, talents and skills needed for the church are always present within the congregation. The pastor-supervisor is to pray for the Holy Spirit to guide him and to open his eyes, that he might truly see; for he will have to tap foundations and stir those who have the necessary gifts.

4. Organizer--(Exodus 18:17-23)

The pastor-organizer is to arrange, set in order, and develop programs and appropriate procedures for specific purposes consistent with the pastor's vision.[57]

5. Enabler--(Ephesians 4:11-12)

The pastor-enabler's task is to equip, enable, and give training and leadership to the members of the congregation to carry out the mission of the church.When Christ ascended to the Father, "he led a host of captives and gave gifts to men." These "gifts" of the Spirit are to enable the church to become a ministering body of Christ.[58]

6. Administrator--(I Corinthians 9:19, 22)

The pastor-administrator administers the affairs of the church by recognizing needs, planning, organizing, staffing, directing, coordinating, communicating and budgeting.[59]

7. Counselor--(Isaiah 1:18)

Pastoral counseling differs from other counseling in one major respect, namely, the inclusion of the religious dimension. The goal of spiritual counseling is to bring men and women into right relationship with God and to lead them into the abundant life. The task of the pastor-counselor is to comfort those who are troubled, give guidance to the perplexed, bring "deliverance to the captives," give assurance of forgiveness to the penitent, give courage to the sick and bereaved, give recovery of sight to the blind and meet the personal needs of the members.[60]

Deacons Understanding the Pastor's Ministry

A pastor is in a very difficult position. His congregation expects him to be an eloquent orator, an ardent student of the Word, an astute administrator and an all-wise counselor. The problem is that no man, however gifted he may be, is capable of doing all those things extremely well. A pastor is to shepherd the flock (1 Peter. 5:2). He is to be the pastor-teacher of his people, to equip them for evangelism and mutual edification.

Because of the time constraints on pastors, many people

attempt to monopolize all of their time and deplete their energy. Therefore, the deacons must understand their pastor's role. **Although the work of the pastor can be most satisfying and rewarding,** it also involves extremely difficult, discouraging and disappointing experiences that can sap the energy and frustrate the efforts of this most dedicated servant of God.

As good soldiers of Christ, many pastors continue without complaint, in spite of the temptation to give up and say, "What's the use anyway?" The work of preaching, the calling and the administrative duties can tax the energies and endurance of a pastor. Physical weariness and nervous exhaustion can result in strained relations between him and his congregation. When misunderstandings and opposition occur involving honest differences of opinion and earnest convictions on the part of respected members, pastors can feel great pressure.[61] The inability to please the very ones he loves the most and the disappointment of being opposed by those he depends on for moral support-- these situations can prompt him, on occasion, to throw up his hands in despair.

Sorry to say, in many churches it seems that the pastor just cannot do anything right. No matter how sincere he may be or how hard he tries, there is always someone that stands ready to find fault and criticize. Someone has described it this way:

- If the pastor is young, he lacks experience; if his hair is gray, he's too old for the young people.

- If he has five or six children, he has too many; if he has none, he's setting a bad example.

- If he preaches from notes, he has canned sermons and is dry; if his messages are extemporaneous, he isn't deep enough.

• If he caters to the poor in the church, he's playing to the grandstand; if he pays attention to the wealthy, he's trying to be an aristocrat.

• If he uses too many illustrations, he's neglecting the Bible; if he does not include stories, he isn't clear.

• If he condemns wrong, he's cranky; if he doesn't preach against sin, he's thought to be a compromiser.

• If he preaches the truth, he's too offensive; if he doesn't present the "whole counsel of God," he's a hypocrite.

• If he fails to please everybody, he's hurting the church and should leave; if he does make them all happy, he has no convictions.

• If he drives an old car, he shames his congregation; if he buys a new one, he's setting his affection on earthly things.

• If he preaches all the time, the congregation gets tired of hearing just one man; if he invites guest ministers, he's shirking his responsibility.

• If he receives a large salary, he's mercenary; if he gets a small one, they say it proves he isn't worth much anyway.

Now, I realize that the previous situations may be exaggerations, but they do emphasize general attitudes in many places. It doesn't seem to make much difference where you go or which church you attend, there's always that one group/faction that is "down" on the pastor. Even though he is doing his very best to shepherd the flock faithfully--longing for the rich blessings of the Lord on his ministry and making an earnest effort to earn the approval of the congregation as a whole--there is always someone who will find fault, oppose him behind his back, or publicly denounce his actions.

Recognizing that such conditions do exist and that they mar the effectiveness of the local church, the deacon must always be there to encourage and help the pastor (Acts 6:1). I am aware that deacons might say they were elected to represent the people in the church, but that is not found anywhere in the Scriptures. Generally, when someone makes a statement like that, they intend to represent the people against the pastor. Too many churches have fought and too many pastors have given up the pastoral ministry because deacons think their appointment gives them a degree of authority over the pastor.

The Gospel of John gives insight into understanding your pastor. The Apostle John wrote:

> There was a man sent from God, whose name was John. This man came for a witness, to bear witness of the Light, that all through him might believe. He was not that Light, but was sent to bear witness of that Light. (John 1:6-8)

Three things are said about John the Baptist that are true for every genuine servant of God. And I am convinced that if these things were kept in mind by each pastor and every member of his congregation, much of the difficulty being experienced in our churches today would be avoided. First, we are told that "there was a man." John was a human being, subject to the same weaknesses and limitations as other people. He was not angel; he was not a supernatural creation; he was not hyper-physical emissary from the throne of God. Rather, as the record states, he was "a man." Second, we are told that John was "a man sent from God." Although he had human limitations, John was distinguished and set apart from others because he was specially chosen--"a man sent from God." Third, we are told that John was sent "to bear witness of the Light." John came to preach Christ, the Light of the world--that was his mission. Verse 8 says, "He was not that Light, but was sent to bear witness to that Light." From this passage in John 1, we learn the following things about John the Baptist:

- He was a man.
- He was sent from God.
- He was to bear witness of the Light.

These very same things can also be said about all pastors who are genuine in their calling. They are men with human limitations, sent from God and given divine authorization. They are men sent from God to bear witness of the Light; they have a heavenly commission. Their primary work is to present the Lord Jesus, the Living word revealed in the written Word. If they hold true to their mission, they will preach Christ. Like John the Baptist, they are to "bear witness of the Light."

So keep in mind these things about this man of God (John) when you think of your pastor:

(1) Is he is born again?

(2) Does he believe the Bible to be the infallible Word of God?

(3) Does he give evidence of being ordained by God?

(4) Is he committed to faithful service and the sound preaching of the Word?

Remember, as a man, he has faults and limitations. As a man with a divine call, however, he should be treated as God's servant. In addition, inasmuch as his mission is to proclaim the Gospel of Christ, you owe him your cooperation and prayer support, to help make his ministry as effective as possible.

In almost **every church, there is at least one group who, although making favorable** comments about the pastor, cannot refrain from publicly pointing out his shortcomings. Because of this, many of God's servants are waging a difficult and discouraging battle. They are doing their best, but because of dissension, dissatisfaction and opposition from those within the church, the work of the Lord is suffering. Now the reason for this, in many instances, is due to a misunderstanding concerning the nature and work of the pastor. It was about Jesus that the Apostle Paul wrote:

> Who, being in the form of God, did not consider it robbery to be equal with God, but made Himself of no reputation, taking the form of a bondservant, and coming in the likeness of men. And being found in appearance as a man, He humbled Himself and became obedient to the point of death, even the death of the cross. (Philippians 2:6-8)

And the Apostle John stated it this way: "And the Word became flesh and dwelt among us" (John 1:14).

Whereas, true ministers of Christ are men sent from God, only the Lord Jesus was the God-man--truly God and man. You may ignore what I say and turn a deaf ear to other preachers, but dare not slight God's Son, the Lord Jesus Christ. He was God Incarnate, the Word made flesh. He came to this world for the purpose of giving Himself as a sacrifice for our sins: "The Son of Man has come to seek and to save that which was lost" (Luke 19:10). Jesus also said, "For even the Son of Man did not come to be served, but to serve, and to give His life a ransom for many" (Mark 10:45). The Apostle Paul told us, "For when we were still without strength, in due time Christ died for the ungoldly…. But God demonstrates His own love toward us, in that while we were still sinners, Christ died for us" (Romans 5:6, 8).

Because the Savior came and provided for our redemption through His death on the cross, salvation is offered as a gift. It is received by faith. The Bible says, "The wages of sin is death, but the gift of God is eternal life in Christ Jesus our Lord" (Romans 6:23). And John gave us this promise: "But as many as received Him, to them He gave the right to become children of God, to those who believe in His name" (John 1:12). To receive Jesus as your Savior, offer this simple prayer of faith right now:

> Lord Jesus, I acknowledge my sinfulness and inability to save myself. But believing that You died and shed Your blood for my sins, I now receive You as my Savior. I'm trusting You alone for my salvation. Save me.

Did you do that? If you did and you really meant what you said, then thank the Lord for saving your soul and claim the promise in Romans 10:13, that "whoever calls on the name of the Lord shall be saved."

Deacons Must Understand the Pastor's Human Limitations

Let's think, first of all, about the fact that all ministers are men. They are restricted and hampered by the very same human limitations as everyone else. The writer in John 1:6, referring to John the Baptist, told us that "there was a man." And in this short phrase, we have a description of all servants of the Lord. God has so ordained that men, in spite of all their faults and shortcomings, should be the channels through which the Word is to be proclaimed to others.

I marvel at God's choice. I never cease to wonder why God called a country boy--a faltering, stumbling, unworthy vessel from across a railroad track in a small town in Alabama--to bear the good news of the Gospel. From the purely human standpoint, He might better have sent angels to minister the Word, or created some special emissaries to proclaim His message. They could have done a perfect job, and then no one could complain or criticize. No one could say, "Oh, he's all right, BUT..." And yet God saw fit to choose men! He saw fit to choose me.

The Lord takes those who are in need of a Savior and places them in positions of privilege to proclaim the glorious message of redemption to others. The Apostle Paul commanded his young friend, Timothy, "And the things that you have heard from me among many witnesses commit these to faithful men who will be able to teach others also" (2 Timothy 2:2).

The fact that pastors are but men, with all the imperfections and characteristics of other human beings, should certainly be evident to everyone. This truth, however, seems to be so easily forgotten when making our demands on their lives and ministry. As a result, too many people in our churches are expecting too much and continually criticizing their preachers with comments such as these: "Oh, our pastor is a wonderful person, BUT..." or "He's a good preacher, but he just doesn't know how to handle people" or "Our pastor is a deep student of the Word, but he's such a poor administrator." Because of this, when a man is called to pastor a church, he's expected to have almost superhuman qualifications:

- He must be a good speaker.
- He must be a deep Bible student.
- He must be a spirited evangelist.
- He must be a compassionate pastor.
- He must have the wisdom of Solomon.
- He must have a pleasing personality and good looks.
- He must be an astute businessman and an effective and efficient administrator.
- He must be creative and original.

And the list goes on. Pity the poor man who fails to live up to all of these requirements. Of him it will be said, "Oh, he has his good points, BUT …"

Some time ago I read an article titled "Qualifications of a Good Pastor," and it further underscored the unreasonable demands often placed on God's servants by deacons and congregations. It reads as follows:

A good pastor must have:

the strength of an ox,
the tenacity of a bulldog,
the daring of a lion,
the wisdom of an owl,
the harmlessness of a dove,
the industry of a beaver,
the gentleness of a sheep,
the versatility of a chameleon.

> the vision of an eagle,
> the hide of a rhinoceros,
> the perspective of a giraffe,
> the endurance of a camel.
> the bounce of a kangaroo,
> the stomach of a horse,
> the disposition of an angel,
> the loyalty of an apostle,
> the faithfulness of a prophet,
> the tenderness of a shepherd,
> the fervency of an evangelist,
> the devotion of a mother,
> and still he could not please everybody!

There are those who would say, "Oh, he's alright, BUT..." Remember, the Bible said that John was "a man." And **as a man, your pastor can't possibly be proficient in all things, nor can he do everything to perfection**. He's going to have his failings and shortcomings simply because God saw fit to use man; and He, in many cases, chooses the weakest of men. The Apostle Paul declared:

> For you see your calling, brethren, that not many wise according to the flesh, not many mighty, not many noble, are called. But God has chosen the foolish things of the world to put to shame the wise, and God has chosen the weak things of the world to put to shame the wise, and God has chosen the weak things of the world to put to shame the things which are mighty; and the base things of the world and the things which are despised God has chosen, and the things which are not, to bring to nothing the

things that are, that no flesh should glory in His presence. (1 Corinthians 1:26-29)

The pastor is called to be a generalist leader. In his leadership role, the pastor serves as a player-coach-enabler. He develops people. As generalist leader the pastor leads the church to determine its spiritual mission. Don't expect your pastor to be perfect or to excel in every area of the ministry. And try not to act so shocked when you discover that he may not be an outstanding Bible teacher, a spirited and effective evangelist, a compassionate pastor, an inspirational preacher, an able administrator and a shrewd businessman, all wrapped up in one. The Lord Himself doesn't demand that much. The Apostle Paul wrote:

> Therefore I run thus: not with uncertainty. Thus I fight: not as one who beats the air. But I discipline my body and bring it into subjection, lest, when I have preached to others, I myself should become disqualified. (1 Corinthians 9:26-27)

With all of these things in mind, then, I would encourage you to pray for your pastor, instead of criticizing him. If, however, you just can't keep your complaints to yourself and you must talk to someone about him, talk to God. And while you're at it, pray for him. If anyone needs the prayers of God's people today, it's the man who labors in the pastorate. I don't know of many other occupations that can be so demanding and yet so discouraging. And I can think of very few professions that offer so many opportunities for failure.

The pastor not only faces the temptations of his own sinful nature and of the world, but also the criticism of unsanctified church members and the hatred of sinners. Because of this, he is a special target of Satan's fiery darts. So pray for him and encourage him. How long has it been since you took your pastor's hand and, with a firm handshake, expressed your gratitude for his ministry? You'd be surprised, even shocked, if you knew how many pastors go on for weeks and months with very little, if any, encouragement. Somehow people get the idea that the preacher doesn't need a good word like others do. But just as you appreciate a "pat on the back" for a job well done, so also your pastor welcomes the expression of your thanks and the assurance of your moral support--not praise that would inflate his ego, but a word of sincerity for his faithful ministry of the Word.

God uses men, with all their shortcomings and failures, "to bear witness of the Light." They need your prayers. They need your encouragement. And they need your help. Is your pastor getting that kind of backing from you? If he's born again, called of God and faithfully preaching the Word, he deserves your loyalty and cooperation. So think about these things, and then be what you should be to your pastor.

Deacons Must Understand the Pastor's Divine Authorization

As discussed earlier, three distinct things were mentioned about John the Baptist. **First**, *he was a man* (John 1:6). He was an earth-born creature with human shortcomings. **Second**, *he was sent from God* (John 1:6). He was different from other men. He was a man all right, but one who was commissioned by the Lord, Himself. Third, *he was sent to preach Christ, the anointed Son of God* (John 1:7).

John's purpose in life was to testify of the Lord Jesus Christ.

And these same three things can be said of every pastor who is born again, called of God, believes the Bible to be the infallible word of God, and is living in obedience to His word. Yes, they are men--they have human limitations. They are men sent from God--they have divine authorization. They are men sent from God to bear witness of the Light--they have a heavenly commission.

Here are a couple of good questions I would ask every deacon: Would you have treated your pastor any differently this week if someone had tipped you off that he was a specially sent 'messenger' from the very throne of God? Would you have criticized your pastor so severely or gossiped about him if you had known that he was chosen and appointed by the Lord himself for the work he is doing? I'm sure many would have to admit that their attitude, actions and words would have been much different toward their pastor if they had been told that God placed him in the church for a definite purpose.

Many servants of God are treated shamefully because we forget that they're men with human weaknesses. They are men sent from God, that is, if they are genuine in their calling. This truth is given to us in John 1. The Apostle wrote:

> There was a man sent from God, whose name was John. This man came for a witness, to bear witness of the Light, that all through him might believe. He was not that Light, but was sent to bear witness of that Light. (John 1:6-8)

The Apostle Paul, one of the greatest preachers the world has ever known, recognized his own shortcomings. In 1 Corinthians 9:27 he said, "But I discipline my body and bring it into subjection, lest, when I have preached to others, I myself should become disqualified." And he also declared in Romans 7, "For I know that in me (that is, in my flesh) nothing good dwells....O wretched man that I am! Who will deliver me from this body of death?" (vv. 18, 24).

Remember these words: "There was a man sent from God." Because your pastor is a man, he needs your prayers and encouragement. And this truth, when applied to the pastor, is what gives us a balanced view of his person and work. If he's seen as only a man, some would surely reason, "Since my pastor is human, like I am, and prone to the same weaknesses and pitfalls, why should I listen to him? He's no better than I am." But **while it's true that he is just a man, it's also a fact that those who have a genuine calling are men sent from God. And as such, they deserve your respect and honor**--not necessarily because they're better, but rather in consideration of their heavenly calling.

This brings us right back, then, to our opening questions: How would you have treated your pastor this past week if you'd been told he was a messenger specially sent from God? Would you have said the things you did about him? Would you have criticized his pulpit manners? Would you have pointed out his poor delivery and grammatical mistakes? Would you have spoken so unkindly to him? When deacons and church members realize that the pastor, in spite of his weaknesses, is a man "sent from God," I'm sure much of the petty criticism in our churches will be eliminated.

Some, however, will certainly reply by saying, "But you don't know our pastor. I wish he were more tactful. At times, he's so poor at expressing himself. He's always got his foot in his mouth. And some of his mannerisms are enough to drive you crazy. You don't know our pastor." Oh yes, I do know him well. You see, I know myself and he's just like me--a man with human weaknesses. But if he's a genuine servant of Christ (as it was said of John the Baptist), then he's a man sent from God and his special "office" calls for your respect. I didn't say he should be worshipped or placed on a clerical pedestal; however, he should be respected because of his calling. Even if you don't respect the man, you must respect the divine office of the man.

In Romans 10, the Apostle Paul made the following comments about those who preach the Gospel.

> How then shall they call on Him in whom they have not believed? And how shall they believe in Him of whom they have not heard? And how shall they hear without a preacher? And how shall they preach unless they are sent? As it is written, How beautiful are the feet of those who preach the gospel of peace, who bring glad tidings of good things! (vv. 14-15)

Although pastors should be treated with respect, there are times, sad to say, when their lives are inconsistent with the teachings of the Scriptures. Some have deliberately violated the precepts of God's Word to the extent that they are bringing an open and public reproach on the cause of Christ. But even if that's the case, no believer should ever engage in a personal crusade against the preacher. Rather, he should quietly and privately deal with the problem in loving concern for the minister himself, and for the work of the Lord. And whatever is done should be bathed in prayer and exercised with the greatest of caution, lest any unjust action is taken against one who is not only a brother in Christ, but also a specially chosen servant of God.

I Samuel 26 tells of the time when David spared the life of King Saul, and this example shows us how careful we should be when dealing with someone appointed by God to a position of trust and responsibility. The Old Testament narrative gives us the setting... David has been chosen to be Israel's next king, but Saul is still on the throne. Motivated by insane jealousy, Saul seeks to kill David, hounding him continually. One evening, David and his company entered Saul's camp while the king lay sound asleep... It was a perfect setup. David could have put his arch enemy out of the way, but he refused to do so. Here is the record of his experience:

> So David and Abishai came to the people by night: and, behold, Saul lay sleeping within the trench, and his spear stuck in the ground at his bolster: but Abner and the people lay round about him. Then said Abishai to David, God hath delivered thine enemy into thine hand this day: now therefore let me smite him, I pray thee, with the spear even to the earth at once, and I will not smite him the second time. And David said to Abishai, Destroy him not, for who can stretch forth his hand against the Lord's anointed, and be guiltless? David said furthermore, As the Lord liveth, the Lord shall smite him; or his day shall come to die; or he shall descend into battle, and perish. The Lord forbid that I should stretch forth mine hand against the Lord's anointed. (1 Samuel 26:7-10)

Now I realize that there is quite a difference between a king of Israel and the pastor of a church. But even as David so highly respected Saul, the Lord's anointed, we should be careful not to stretch forth a hand unjustly against any "man sent from God." Deacons should never wage war, or fight against the man of God.

I can still imagine deacons saying, however, "My pastor just isn't doing the job. The church is suffering. He should leave. How can we handle a situation like that? I do respect him and wouldn't want to hurt him for anything." The following points are from an article printed in a church bulletin. They may be helpful to any deacon struggling with getting rid of his pastor.

1. Look the pastor straight in the eye while he's preaching and say "Amen" once in a while, and he'll preach himself to death.

2. Pat him on the back and brag on his good points, and he'll probably work himself to death.

3. Rededicate your life to Christ and ask the preacher for some job to do, preferably winning some lost person to Christ, and he'll die of heart failure.

4. Get the church to unite in prayer for the preacher and he'll soon become so effective that a larger church will take him off your hands.

If only congregations would pray for their pastors and show respect for them as men sent from God, many problems could be avoided. The church would have a better image in the community, and children would have a more favorable attitude toward the work of the Gospel.

How many times have I heard people say, "I just don't understand why children have so little interest in the church now that they've grown up. They just don't seem to care about going anymore." After all the criticism they've heard, is it any wonder? Sunday after Sunday they've had "roast pastor" for dinner. His sermons were torn apart, his pulpit manners laughed at and his appearance and dress ridiculed by their parents. And then we're surprised when little children don't have any regard for the church or the preacher! If you have children in the home, be careful about criticizing the pastor in their presence. It's your duty, as faithful parents, to cultivate respect in the minds of your little ones, for the office of those men who are sent from God to serve as undershepherds of the flock. So don't forget, your pastor is a man ... a man sent from God ... a man sent to bear witness of the Light.

Let me say this special word to you if you have never accepted Jesus Christ as your Savior: as long as you look at man, you're bound to be disappointed. Even the preacher, although sent from God, is subject to human failures. There is One, however, in whom there is no disappointment. He is the Lord Jesus Christ, the God-man. He alone, of all men, lived a perfect life. He was absolutely sinless and did not need to die as other men, yet He assumed our guilt. He went to the cross, He shed His blood for our sins, He was raised from the dead. And now forgiveness of sin and life everlasting can be yours if you'll acknowledge your guilt and trust Him for salvation. The Bible says:

> If you confess with your mouth the Lord Jesus, and believe in your heart that God has raised Him from the dead, you will be saved. For with the heart, one believes unto righteousness, and with the mouth, confession is made unto salvation. (Romans 10:9-10)

Deacons Must Understand the Heavenly Commission

Yes, John the Baptist was a man--he had *human limitations*.

He was a man sent from God--he had *divine authorization*. He was sent from God to bear witness of the Light--he had a *heavenly commission*. He was to preach Christ. These three things are also true of all genuine ministers of the Gospel today. As men, they are subject to human weaknesses and failings, and they, therefore, need our prayers. As men sent from God, they deserve our respect and should be esteemed because of their divine appointment. Like John, their calling is *to bear witness of the Light*.

Even as the work of John the Baptist was to bear witness of the Light, so today the work of those who are sent from God is to present Christ. That, of course, is best accomplished through the faithful preaching of the word of God. **Expounding the Word must take priority over everything else in the life of those called "to bear witness of the Light."** Anything that hinders them from this task--anything that detracts from their effectiveness in presenting Christ, the Living Word, through the written Word must be carefully avoided.

The high priority that should be given to the ministry of the Word by those servants called of God to preach is made very clear in Acts 6. In this passage we read about a situation in the early church which, if not handled correctly, could have sidetracked the Apostles.

> Now in those days when the number of the disciples was multiplying, there arose a complaint against the Hebrews by the Hellenists, because their widows were neglected in the daily distribution. (Acts 6:1)

Very likely, "the daily distribution" had reference to the distribution of money and food to widows in the Jerusalem church.

And here's what they did about the problem: "Then the twelve summoned the multitude of the disciples and said, 'It is not desirable that we should leave the Word of God and serve tables'" (v. 2).

As conscientious men, they could not ignore the plight of those poor widows. You see, serving tables wasn't what they had been called to do. It was their responsibility to give themselves to prayer and the Word. (We must understand that the enemy desires to distance the pastor from prayer and study of the Word.) The Apostles didn't consider themselves too good or too important to serve tables, but they recognized that this was not the ministry to which God had called them. So please notice what they did. Oh that we might learn a lesson from this!

> Therefore, brethren, seek out from among you seven men of good reputation, full of the Holy Spirit and wisdom, whom we may appoint over this business; but we will give ourselves continually to prayer and to the ministry of the Word. (Acts 6:3-4)

Seven spiritual men who could be trusted were appointed to oversee the needs of the widows so that the teaching elders might "give [themselves] continually to prayer and to the ministry of the Word." Having properly delegated the responsibility of meeting the physical needs of the people to the deacons, the Apostles, as men "sent from God" to "bear witness of the Light," gave themselves wholly to their task of praying and preaching. And, as a result, God blessed in a wonderful way. Verse 7 tells us that "the Word of God spread, and the number of disciples multiplied greatly in Jerusalem, and a great many of the priests were obedient to the faith."

And today, **whenever you find a church with a born-**

again, dedicated pastor who gives himself faithfully to prayer, study and the ministry of the Word, you'll discover a spiritual, vibrant, growing congregation. But when a congregation places such exacting demands on its leader, insisting he officiate every committee meeting, attend all fellowship functions and be active in a myriad of civic affairs, to the extent that his prayer and Bible study time is interrupted, you'll find a church that is either lukewarm and lethargic, or cold and dead. A church may be filled with activity and have a big program, but that doesn't necessarily mean it's producing fruit for eternity. It is possible for a church to have numerous activities, meetings, clubs, projects and many "wheels going around," without really doing anything, as far as its intended work is concerned.

When I look at some congregations, I am reminded of an impressive machine that has hundreds of cogs, gears, pulleys, and belts which all go around smoothly and swiftly at the touch of a button. When the inventor, however, is asked about the function of the machine and what it is supposed to do, he replies, "Oh, it isn't supposed to do anything, but doesn't it run beautifully?"

So, too, when you attend a church where the Word is neglected, Christ is not preached and the pastor is loaded down with administrative responsibilities, you may witness a large organization with many "wheels going around" but no spiritual power being generated. Be sure, therefore, to put first things first. Make certain your pastor isn't burdened down with administrative and civic obligations to the extent that his spiritual life suffers and the ministry of the Word does not remain central in his life (and in the church).

John the Baptist came to "bear witness of the Light." Your pastor, too, should be occupied with preaching Christ. And, if he's to do so effectively, don't expect him to be the church errand boy, drive the Sunday school bus, run off the church bulletins, do the janitorial work, take various members to all of their meetings, preside at every function or be out on visitation every afternoon and evening. All of these things are good, and every pastor who is genuinely sent from God would be glad to perform whatever services he can. But both you and he must be on guard lest these activities prevent him from fulfilling his primary mission. Not only will he slip spiritually, but the entire church many well go down with him. Remember, the spiritual tone of a congregation is keyed to its pastor.

So when you are asked to do something for which you're qualified, and time and circumstances allow, don't say, "Let the pastor do it--that's what he's getting paid for." Rather, do your part and help the man "sent from God," so that he can more effectively "bear witness of the Light." Every deacon should want to help his pastor in such a way that together they can fulfill the work of the church. The elderly need attention, the spiritually indifferent need to be warned and counseled, the poor need companionship, the sorrowful need comfort and cheer. Your pastor can't do all these things. Both he and the church need you. Together, you can do great things for God.

This point bears repeating: Whenever you're asked to do anything for which you're qualified, you should give it serious consideration. And, if it can be handled without detriment to your family or without causing you to neglect other responsibilities of equal or greater importance, do it. God will bless you if it's done in His name and for His glory. Help in whatever way you can, so that your pastor may be free to perform his ministry in the manner God desires.

Dr. John H. Walker

CHAPTER FOUR

ESTABLISHING A BIBLICAL RELATIONSHIP BETWEEN THE PASTOR & DEACON IN THE BLACK BAPTIST CHURCH

One of the strongest misconceptions about the job of the deacon is the amount of influence and power he thinks he has.[62] The contention and strife that have grown from this mentality in the Black Church has its roots in the deacon-of-old, who was often considered to be the boss. He gave the orders, and his board held the power. If one wanted anything, including the pastor, he had to get permission from the deacon board. The chief problem that resulted in the Black Church was that the deacon was looked upon, by his brother, as the church's overlord and not that of a spiritual undershepherd. A serious indictment against the churches of years past is that they put powerful men in office to serve as deacons, instead of men that were power-filled by the Holy Ghost and considered it a privilege to serve. It is not about being powerful, but power-filled. The problem has extended itself to these modern times in which we live. How did this confusion over the office of the deacon in the Black

Baptist Church begin? The very stronghold of the black community has been the Black Church. It is still our most stabilizing agent for inspiring and sustaining spiritual and social change. Our church roots, as well as our beliefs, stem from our African heritage. Reactions against injustices have produced great areas of focus and self-expression for the black man in his or her church. Having found himself jobless, and in many cases homeless, he was often abused and made to stoop to his former master(s).[63] He was disenfranchised and minimized by the so-called liberators of the North. The black man, no matter how affluent he tried to be, was humiliated and had his rights reduced to those of a second class citizen. The only place he could speak (and can still speak) his peace was in the Black Church.

The ministry of the deacon can best be understood as we look at its past meaning and significance.[64] **First**, we must understand that the office of the deacon is a Scriptural one (Acts 6:1-10). Modern men have sought to exploit and destroy the office, and its meaning. Many have fought for the deacon to have absolute control of the inner workings and administration of the Black Church. This may be a noble desire, but it is certainly not Scriptural. In rural areas, where the pastor rides a circuit (or pastors more than one church), it may be desirable to have men to do the day-to-day business. But, there ought to be some imposed limitations upon the extent to which a deacon can speak and act on behalf of the church without the its approval.

> "God did not save you to be a sensation. He saved you to be a servant."
> *John E. Hunter*

Because some freewheeling deacons operate without restraint, some shady, underhanded deals have been made, to the hurt of churches across the country. It is safe to say that many pastors' ministries have been ruined because of the deacons. Against the pastor's better judgement, and the dismay of the church, deacons have been placed on boards simply because they look like good men to have. However, an undue amount of trouble generally occurs.[65] Any church that has deacons who do not meet the Bible qualifications, recorded in Acts 6:1-10, will have problems, sooner or later. If the pastor is going to have a **Biblical relationship** with the deacons, he must make sure that he scrutinizes each individual closely, so there will be a minimum of problems and difficulties. The most important requirement of a deacon is that he be qualified. A deacon cannot be all that God wants him to be unless he, too, meets the biblical qualifications. Therefore, it would be better for a church not to have deacons if no one can meet the qualifications.

Many deacons have lofty ideas about being the greatest deacon that ever lived.[66] Their idea of greatness is to leave behind a legacy that all men can look up to with pride and say, "There was a deacon who really threw his weight around: when he spoke, even the pastor would tiptoe lightly." However, this idea of greatness does not compare with the way our Lord saw greatness. He said, "Whosoever of you will be the chiefest, shall be servant of all" (Mark 10:44). For a man to properly comprehend the potential that the Lord demands him to reach, he must be a servant. If you want to be the greatest, you must first be a deacon (servant).[67] The word "deacon," which comes from the Greek word diakonos, is used thirty times in the Greek New Testament, but only on five occasions is it translated as "deacon" in the King James Version. When not translated "deacon," diakonos is translated "ministers" or "servants." Diakonos literally means "through dust." Although the origin of the word is questioned, the concept of raising dust suggests a servant hastening to serve or to wait on his master.

Deacons have usually risen in influence and position in the Black Church according to seniority, pastoral appointment, educational opportunities, specialized training, mothers wit, jungle smarts, self-assertion and the ability to perform well at several levels.[68] However, the word of God lists personal qualifications for deacons. Pastors and deacons cannot have a biblical relationship without meeting the **Biblical Qualifications** (refer to Chapter 2). The last Bible qualification, and by no means the least to adhere to, is of course mentioned in Acts 6:3 and 1 Timothy 3:9-11--that is, the trait of loyalty.

We expect our deacons to be loyal--loyal to the church, loyal to the pastor, loyal to the program of the church and loyal to what God is doing through the church and through the pastor. Don't you see? The deacons were originally chosen by God to help the pastor, to lift up his hands and to serve him. When a deacon ceases to be loyal to the church program and the pastor whom God has called, then he ceases to fulfill the main purposes of the office.

Pre-Ministry Training

The road to a good relationship between pastor and deacon begins with meeting spiritual qualifications, as discussed in Chapter 2. Much of the contention between pastor and deacon, in the Black Baptist Church, stems from a lack of **pre-ministry training**. Traditionally, there are many persons chosen because of a lack of able bodies; however, they lack informative preparation.[69] Those selected to serve in the diaconate are generally persons with good intentions for the work at hand. After a period of time, without informative preparation, they begin to view their roles as vanguards of the spiritual welfare of the church.

Their sense of service changes to a sense of privileged authority, thus creating a power struggle between the pastor and deacons.

For many years, in the Black Baptist Church, there has been a constant conflict with the diaconate over power and authority. Pre-ministry preparation is essential to establishing a biblical relationship with pastor and deacon.[70] A person can possess all the characteristics that Acts 6 suggests, and still not be prepared for deacon-ship. There is a need for preparation and training. The purpose is twofold: **(1)** to help deacons understand their responsibility as deacons and **(2)** to equip deacons for their assignments in the church's pastoral ministries. In the Black Baptist Church, we have been ruled for too long by money and ignorance. A trained deacon will be an asset to his church and pastor. Training is a continual process. Many pastors have established training for six months to a year. Training will greatly impact a deacon's ministry, and each pastor can choose what works best for him and the "diaconate." However, at the Macedonia Baptist Church, where I serve as senior pastor, there is a training compartment built into each monthly meeting. Churches should require training for deacons before placing them in positions. We will now examine several areas that a deacon should be trained in, to establish and maintain a biblical relationship with the pastor.

Church Polity and Policy

Church polity and policy is an area that creates much tension between pastor and deacon.[71] Many deacons feel as though they are the governing body of the Black Baptist Church, while other Baptist churches operate by congregational vote. The method of government may vary from church to church. One church may elect to trust their pastor and deacons to handle the day-to-day functions of administration, while another may decide to appoint various committees and groups to handle the workload. Whatever the process, the Black Baptist Church, however, is an autonomous body. The government rests in the hands of the people, and not just the deacons. Deacons must be taught the polity and policies of the church they are serving. No two churches are alike, neither are any two pastors exactly alike in their administration.

The church is an organism more so than an organization, as such it has a body more than that of a structure. The Body has many members, and Jesus Christ is the Head (See 1 Corinthians 12:27-28 and Ephesians 4:4-16). Deacons must have an understanding concerning church membership. They must understand that membership is acquired by a person's Profession of Faith (the acceptance of Jesus Christ as their Lord and Savior); and then followed by baptism, by letter (the moving of their membership from another church) and by Christian Experience. Their profession of faith acknowledges that they already belong to the body of Christ. One is usually received this way when the local church they belonged to is no longer in existence, or the records are unavailable. A person can also join under watchcare. This allows a person living in an area for a short period of time to be part of a particular church family while they are there.

Deacons must have an understanding of money. The Lord's Church is to be financed by *tithes* and offering pledge commitments *(free will offerings)*. There is NO other way to finance God's house (See Malachi 3:10; Matthew 23:23; Luke 6:38; 2 Corinthians 9:6-8). They must also understand mission and benevolence. Our mission endeavor is to feed the hungry, clothe the naked, visit the sick, go to the prisons, care for the widows and orphans in their affliction, relieve the poor and give a cup of cold water in Jesus' name. (See Matthew 25:31-46; James 1:27; 1 John 3:16-18).

Deacons should know the proper procedures for Baptism (Colossians 2:12) and the Lord's Supper (1 Corinthians 11:24-34). The baptistery should be properly prepared, making sure the water is clean and the temperature is right. The deacons are to assist the pastor in and out of the pool, and in helping to prepare the candidates. I believe that the Lord's Supper should not be sloppy or out of order. It should be carried out with the utmost reverence and respect. Deacons should know their place and position--before the ceremony. Most commonly, deacons are positioned around the table, on the right and left side of the pastor. Dark suits are the preferable attire in the winter; light colors and white gloves in the summer. The clothes do not alter the essence, but they do alter the expression.

Deacons should move with uniformity. The deaconesses should help with the preparation of elements, table, pulpit and sanctuary. Cleanliness, sacredness and holiness are to be maintained at all times. Time spent together in training can help bring harmony, in the event that confusion arises about "the way we use to do things with the other pastor." Deacons should learn that pastors adapt their programs to fit the needs of the local congregation they are serving.

Knowledge of the Bible

The deacons in any church should have a general working knowledge of the Bible; any man chosen for service should be trained to rightly divide the word of truth.[72] He should be able to handle the word of God so effectively that when he is called upon to counsel others--either as the pastor's assistant in a session, or in the pastor's absence--he will be confident in speaking the truth wisely. The pastor will not hesitate in recommending him, and the people involved will go away refreshed, enlightened and praising God that such a person exists who can be trusted to tell them what the Lord has said.

A deacon should know the Word and be trained in the doctrines of the Baptist Church. He should know what he believes, and the reason for such beliefs. The deacon should also understand the nature and work of other Christian denominations so that he will not be held suspect as a heretic for introducing some new doctrine. It should be said of every deacon that their footing is firm and that they stand confidently assured of their Scriptural and doctrinal teachings.

Visitation

The deacons should be trained in the area of visitation. The main reason for visitation is that it helps to maintain a solid communion of believers who are concerned about each other.[73] The church had support in the days of Peter and John and the other apostles. Not only did they hear the word, pray, sing, break bread together and witness, they were also concerned about meeting each other's needs (Acts 2:44). The caring and sharing process was so selfless (Philippians 2:3-5) that no one within the church ever lacked for anything (Acts 4:24-35).

The deacons must be trained to be responsible for knowing the whole membership through visitation and communication. They should make it their goal to know all the members by name, no matter what the size of the congregation. At the church I serve, we operate under a deacon-family ministry plan. Each deacon and wife team is assigned several families in the church. These family teams visit, are friends with and are available to the families whenever called upon. This plan has proven to be a blessing to me as well as to the membership. However, deacons must be cautious not to become dictators, or try to convince families that they are the only ones they can turn to in times of trouble, or try to rally support for petty battles that they want to wage against the church and the pastor. The deacons should be taught to do the Lord's business--and then leave. Deacons must know the why and how-to of visitation. They need to visit the hospitals, the nursing homes and the bereaved. Deacons must make personal visits, dress appropriately and be sensitive to various situations. They need to listen to what is being said by the members and keep reports of the visits. They must be mindful not to smoke, make false promises or gossip. Deacons are sometimes called upon to accompany the pastor on a visit or to be present during a counseling session. The deacon should be trained to understand that they should not betray confidences.

The Amount of Power

I believe much time should be placed on stressing to deacons the extent of their power. Deacons should know how far to go and when to quit.[74] Their job description and specific duties should be spelled out, and they should know when it is time to call the pastor. The deacon's office is characterized not only by spiritual inspiration but also by a concentration of wisdom that strengthens their effectiveness. The pastor has accepted the place of leadership. The only other officers in the New Testament churches were deacons. In Acts Chapter 6, the Apostles said, "Look ye out among you seven men of honest report, full of the Holy Ghost and wisdom, whom we may appoint over this business" (v. 3). They were to work under the Apostles in looking after poor widows and others who needed help. So, deacons are servants of the church to work under the pastor. They are the pastor's helpers.

Deacons who embrace the pastor's vision can help the congregation see where the pastor is going.[75] Deacons must be careful to use their influence for the glory of God, and not for the promotion of self-interests. God has entrusted them to follow leadership, and they should do their utmost to lead the way in following. This will make them strong, the church more harmonious and the pastor eternally grateful that he has men who want to make his job easier. I suggest that the training of deacons be revealed to the church.[76] This will remind the church of the deacon's commitment to the ministry and his training.

Team Ministry--A Shared Ministry

The deacons and pastor must lead the church, together. Therefore, their relationship must be a partnership. A good sign of a team ministry in action is evident in Acts 6:5-7. The first sign is the acceptance of the plan of action by the membership. When a plan for ministry is presented to the whole congregation, the members will delight in the effort. This plan, which must be accepted by all, enables the church to continue its growth. Effective teamwork between pastor and deacon allows the preacher to preach and the deacons to help. Jesus knew and applied the team principle. He formed a team of twelve men and trained them to carry on His work after His return to heaven. To establish a biblical relationship with pastor and deacon, there must be a team concept. It should be understood that there is work to be done; therefore, both must use the gifts and talents they have to serve each other, as well as the congregation.

The pastor and deacon share similar qualifications which are not set by man. God gave divine insight to Paul as he set forth qualities of spiritual life that both pastor and deacon are to possess. There is always grave danger lurking nearby when the church lowers the qualifications for either the deacon or pastor. 1 Timothy 3 speaks of the kind of person both leaders are to be. They are to be spiritual men on a spiritual mission. Both pastor and deacon must see each other in the process of becoming.

Understand Each Other's Ministry

The church calls the pastor to be a generalist leader. In his leadership role the pastor leads the church to determine its spiritual mission. Deacons are exemplary leaders. They serve as models for fellow Christians to follow and are to set a good example before the congregation. Their personal habits should not bring reproach upon the Lord or His church. However, deacons often serve behind the scenes, out of the spotlight or central focus of activities, while the pastor is in the spotlight. This can create jealousy and contention between the pastor and deacons. I personally believe that if the deacons and the pastor are going to have a biblical relationship, it must be biblically based. Paul the Apostle gave the church of Corinth a very splendid exhortation in 1 Corinthians 10:11: "Now all these things happened unto them for examples: and they are written for our admonition, upon whom the ends of the world are come."

And if we in the church today can learn anything, I believe it should be from the Scriptures. We must remember that God never called a committee, **board** or organization to do His work. God calls <u>men</u>, and in the Scriptures, these prophets, evangelists, pastors, etc., have been placed by God as the leaders in any "given" circumstance. For the deacons and the people in the church to have the right relationship, they both must recognize and be obedient to the pastor's place of authority.

> Remember them which have the rule <u>over</u> <u>you</u>, who have spoken unto you the word of God; whose faith follow considering the end of the conversation…. Obey them that have the rule over you, and submit yourselves; for they watch for your souls, as they that must give account, that they may do it with joy, and not with grief; for that is unprofitable for you. Salute all them that have the rule over you, and all the saints. (Hebrews 13:7, 24)

The greatest example of a servant's attitude in relation to his leader is found in 1 Samuel 26:7-11.[77] (See earlier reference in Chapter 3.) David had a prime opportunity to get rid of King Saul--once and for all--but he would not touch God's anointed. David seems to say, "No, sir! Even though Saul is all wrong and has grievously shamed me, and I have justifiable reasons to put him to death, for this one reason I won't do it: This man is the Lord's anointed." I like what David said in verse ten of the same chapter: "As the Lord liveth, the Lord shall smite him, or his day shall come to die; or he shall descend into battle and perish." David is saying, "Let's keep our hands off, for he's the Lord's anointed. Let's leave him in God's hands, for God will take care of him--forever."

Today, those who are serious, genuine servants of God are His "anointed" ones, in the sense that they are specially chosen vessels of God to bear witness of the Light. The deacon's attitude toward the man of God should be the same as David's attitude toward King Saul. Although the pastor may be wrong, deacons should be willing to say, with David, "Destroy him not; for who can stretch forth his hand against the Lord's anointed, and be guiltless?" (1 Samuel 26:9).

To establish this biblical relationship, the deacons should not expect the pastor to be perfect.[78] Don't expect him to be able to do everything. Don't expect him to be an outstanding Bible teacher, a spirited evangelist, a compassionate pastor, and an inspiring teacher, all in one; for even God himself doesn't expect that. In John 1:6 it states that "there was a man," not an angel, not a divine being, not a supernatural person. God saw fit to choose a man with human limitations, to bear witness of the Light.

In ministry, anyone can experience tension. However, we're called to be holy and to provide an example of righteousness living for those we lead. On the other hand, we're human, and unable to completely live up to our calling. Therefore, the pastor and deacon must realize that they are constantly in the becoming stage. Every chosen servant has been endowed with a special gift and a particular ministry. If we want God's fullest blessings, we should recognize the gift of God in our pastor and not act so disillusioned and surprised if he or she fails in other respects. Acknowledge the gift that God has given.

Steps to a Biblical Relationship with Your Pastor

Place yourself in the pastor's shoes, and try to experience what he feels as he goes about his work each day! Being a pastor is like many other tasks in life, and yet it is unlike anything else in the world. It is about being loved and unloved, wanted and unwanted, understood and misunderstood. It is heaven and, to be honest, a little bit of hell, at times. The pastor is a man, just like you. He needs a friend at times. He needs someone who will keep his confidences and share with him during moments of loneliness.

Deacons should pray with and for the pastor. As you go about your daily work, breathe a silent prayer of Thanksgiving for him and his ministry. Mention his name in your private and public prayers. Stop by the pastor's office sometimes, not just to talk, but for the sole purpose of joining him in prayer. It is a good policy for pastor and deacon to set aside a definite time to just pray together. This is a good way to lay a solid biblical foundation in your relationship.

Deacons need to affirm the pastor. Deacons will be affirmed as they affirm and support the pastor.[79] Urge the congregation to do certain things for the pastor, such as provide adequate compensation for him (including salary, housing, car allowance, annuity and other benefits). Free him from a never-ending flow of activities so that he can have deserved time with his family in recreation, with God in personal devotion, and with his books in study. Help him stay mentally stimulated by providing conference and convention time, buying materials for his library and offering him opportunities in continuing theological education. When deacons take the leadership in affirming the pastor, they are saying, "Pastor, we love you."

The Deacon must support the pastor because the deacon is the pastor's moral and spiritual helper in service to the people. He should be supportive of his pastor publicly and privately. Encourage him, defend him when he is criticized unfairly, be frank with him when it is thought that he is mistaken; but whatever the case, support and stand with the pastor. To establish and maintain a biblical relationship between pastor and deacon, there must be fellowship.[80] Enjoy fellowship with your pastor, and rejoice that your partnership means he can depend on you. Practice being open, honest and loving, in all your relationships.

Deacons are expected to be men of integrity, consecration and wisdom. They should be intelligent regarding their duties and in full sympathy with the policies of their leader.

I would urge every deacon to never publicize his pastor's faults. Don't go around criticizing and gossiping; however, if you must talk about him, talk to God. Tell the Lord about him and then leave it with Him. There are many pastors who go for weeks and months without the slightest bit of encouragement. Somehow folks think the preacher doesn't need encouragement like other people do. Remember, even as you like encouragement when you have done a job to the best of your ability, your pastor also would rejoice in an expression of your appreciation and confidence ... not praise that would inflate his ego and pride, but a word of thanks for his faithful ministry. How long has it been since you took your pastor by the hand and, shaking it firmly, expressed your gratitude for his ministry?

The relationship between the pastor and deacons should be one of complete trust, confidence and union--one that is similar to those in the first church (Acts 2:46).[81] Deacons are to provide friendship and be a source of encouragement to the pastor.

> "The only people who will be really happy are those who have sought and found how to serve."
>
> *Albert Schweitzer*

Dr. John H. Walker

CHAPTER FIVE

THE WORK OF THE NEW TESTAMENT DEACON

The ministry of deacons has changed somewhat from the original ministry of Acts 6. It was, is and always will be, until Jesus comes, for the deacons to be assistants to the pastor (Acts 6:34). The deacons must always remember that they are the arms of the pastor, and they are to assist him in ministering to the congregation. Deacons should never be poisoned by traditional mindsets that hinder church growth. I understand that duties for deacons vary from church to church. However, a fresh look will reveal that the deacons were chosen to help the pastor. Some will say the deacons were elected to represent the people in the church. The deacons were never elected to represent the people. Acts 6:1-4 makes it plain that the Apostles (pastors) were too busy serving tables and giving daily ministration to the poor, to fulfill their spiritual calling: preaching and praying.

In Acts 6:5, the Apostle said, "Look ye out among you seven men of honest report, full of the Holy Ghost and wisdom, whom we may appoint over this business." That is, they were to work under the Apostles in looking after poor widows and others who needed help. Therefore, deacons are servants of the church, called to work under the pastor. There is no indication in the Bible that deacons ever had any place of authority over the preacher, the church, the building or the finances. The office of the deacon is one of servitude and should be exercised in humility, with a clear conscience and with heavenly wisdom. The only reason deacons have been given authority in the local church is because the people refused to abide by the word of God. **There is only one authority in the local church and that is the pastor. His voice is to be heard and respected "as having the watch-care" for the souls of the people in the church. His authority is to be respected and obeyed in all matters**, <u>even if he is wrong</u>; for no one has the right to oppose a pastor in matters of spiritual guidance, unless done according to Scripture (see 1 Timothy 5:19-20). The pastor may be wrong, but he is still pastor. And, if we believe the Bible, then the Holy Ghost has made him overseer of the flock (Acts 20:28). **To lay hands on God's man before God has taken His hands off is sin, and will be dealt with by God, accordingly.**[82]

Many pastors have cried and thrown their hands up in utter confusion and shock because their deacon board voted to get rid of them. Many pastors have spent countless nights in tears, pleading with the people to turn to Christ and live right. Many pastors have forsaken homes, loved ones and friends to obey the LORD as His man. They've preached sermon after sermon to redeem the lost. They've married sons and daughters, buried mothers and fathers, and dedicated babies. They found that the ones they've loved have turned their backs on them and asked them to leave. What a pity--what a shame and disgrace to the Lord Jesus Christ (who gave us His Word as authority to follow and adhere to) that we cannot obey Him.

Churches that allow deacons to have that type of power

usually die or just linger on with no Holy Spirit power to change lives. Deacons have no authority of any kind unless the pastor gives them authority. The deacons may serve on an advising ministry or team, but never on a board. The organized, true church has a pastor, deacons and people that are willing to serve. We must tear down boards. Dr. George McCalep, in his book *Sin in the House*, says, "Boards operate according to the letter of the law, and the church should operate according to the spirit of love."[83]

I caution that **there is no need to change the name of your board to Deacon's Ministry, Armorbearer, Deaconship or Diaconate if you are still going to operate like a board**. The seven men chosen in Acts 6 were not called deacons until later (Philippians 1:1). **The contents went in before the label went on. Many churches need to change the contents before changing the names**. It is necessary to reinitiate the deacons serving as an advisory ministry or team. Their task, as an advisory group, is to help advise the pastor on matters--at his request. Too many deacons come to deacon's meetings, church, etc., for the sole purpose of cornering the pastor, in order to tell him how the church should be run. Actually, those deacons are only agitating and upsetting the pastor.

Deacons do not have the right or the authority to tell the pastor what to do or to demand things from the him (1 Timothy 5:1). Now this doesn't mean that one cannot discuss important issues with the pastor or bring matters to his attention. For, if the pastor is a man that desires to have the kind of church that would be pleasing to the Lord, he will usually ask for the deacons' advice. But if the pastor is certain he has the mind of God and does not ask the deacons what they think, it does not mean the pastor doesn't care or is trying to slide something by. It simply means he doesn't desire to have advice or comments on that particular subject. So what should be the deacon's attitude in this matter? The same as it was in Bible times. They should pray that God would use the pastor in whatever decision he makes, and should never discuss the situation with other people.

Read Numbers 16:1-50. This account tells of Moses, God's chosen leader. Although God had appointed Moses to lead His people, the sons of Levi found fault with him. They began to speak out against Moses, and God destroyed 14,950 of them that day. **It is a serious sin to speak out against God's man (See 1 Chronicles 16:22 and Psalm 105:15).** Deacons should be willing to help the pastor in any area of work, without murmuring or complaining. Also, deacons should not have to be asked to help--all the time. They should be asking, "Pastor, do you need my help? I'll be glad to do whatever you need." Deacons must help the pastor in the teaching, preaching and the evangelizing of souls outside as well as inside the church.

In too many churches, deacons are more concerned about trying to watch, control or get one up on the pastor. I contend that a church will grow if deacons perform their duties in daily ministration. **Daily ministration makes one a deacon.**[84] If a deacon will be honest with himself and true to his ministry, he/she really doesn't have time to be genuinely focused and available to perform other duties or services. When other duties are assigned to the deacon, they should truly be contributing to **(1)** the purpose of the church and **(2)** the helping and assisting of the pastor in his ministries. There should not be conflicts between the daily ministration and other duties assigned to the deacon (if his schedule is well thought out). If there is conflict, however, daily ministration should never be sacrificed. In the life of the deacon, one can, and sometimes will, be called upon to perform other services; but he must be mindful that he is ALWAYS a deacon first. It's okay to perform other services, but not at the expense of the daily ministration.

Daily ministration is the ministry of serving, helping, aiding, and waiting on people, with haste.[85] In other words, deacons are to lovingly and respectfully take care of people--meeting their needs immediately. To remain a true deacon, daily ministration must be performed. No person can independently decide to become a deacon, and then put himself in the position--he must be chosen by others.

When people have been ministered to, their dignity and integrity MUST be left intact; if not, it certainly should not be the result of any inappropriate act or behavior on the part of the deacon. Every deacon should be held accountable for his assigned responsibilities. A deacon's performance should be tracked and kept on record. This record can be used as a performance tool to give the deacon feedback. Yes, someone needs to monitor the deacon's performance. If a deacon is not performing daily ministration, the matter must be addressed. Lack of or inadequate performance should not go unnoticed--or unaddressed. People's lives are being affected.[86] Matthew 18:15-17 shares the appropriate process to be followed when a brother is found at fault, or in error:

MOREOVER IF THY BROTHER SHALL TRESPASS AGAINST THEE, GO AND TELL HIM HIS FAULT BETWEEN THEE AND HIM ALONE: IF HE SHALL HEAR THEE, THOU HAST GAINED THY BROTHER. BUT IF HE WILL NOT HEAR THEE, THEN TAKE WITH THEE ONE OR TWO MORE, THAT IN THE MOUTH OF TWO OR THREE WITNESSES EVERY WORD MAY BE ESTABLISHED. AND IF HE SHALL NEGLECT TO HEAR THEM, TELL IT

UNTO THE CHURCH: BUT IF HE SHALL NEGLECT TO HEAR THE CHURCH, LET HIM BE UNTO THEE AS A HEATHEN MAN AND PUBLICAN. (*Emphasis added*)

A deacon is a deacon as long as he functions. This is based on the will/choice of the deacon--not the lack of ability to perform. When a deacon does not function, the needs of the people he's been assigned to take care of are not being met. The cost of "saving face" or doing nothing, in order not to bring attention to the deacon, is too high. Which issue is more important? Which holds the most value--a non-functioning deacon saving face, or getting the needs of the people met?

When an individual no longer has the desire or will to serve as a deacon, for whatever reason, he should be able to walk away without guilt.[87] More than we care to admit, there are deacons that would like to serve in some other capacity, but are trapped by tradition. That is why it is so important that deacons serve on rotation. They feel that they cannot change their area of service with their honor, dignity and integrity intact; as though it's a disgrace or dishonor to change services once you have started. So the diaconate ends up with (1) a non-functioning deacon holding a title, (2) negative representation, (3) negative press and (4) another negative hit on its reputation. No wonder there are those that are asking: "Why is the deacon needed in today's church?" Not everybody (including some current deacons) should be a deacon. There is no shame in not being a deacon.[88] Many different services can be rendered to God and mankind. One type of service has no more or less value than another, in God's vineyard. They are all important, and the rewards are the same.

Deacons are not the mediators between the pastor and congregation. Deacons were never intended to be mediators, that is for Jesus Christ. It is, however, their responsibility to see that there is order in the congregation while the man or woman of God is preaching the word of God. Too often deacons are the authors of confusion. I have shared this observation with deacons during their training sessions: "Deacons, you have two buckets in your hand for any situation in the church. One is filled with water and the other with gasoline. Which one will you use?" Having worked as a firefighter for ten years, I am well acquainted with what gasoline will do to a fire. Many fires break out in a congregation. It is the deacon's job to be a peacemaker and not a peace breaker.

Deacons are Not the People's Voice

I have heard too many deacons say they are speaking for the people. One must be mindful that the pastor speaks for the people. Deacons must understand that they are not there to stand against the pastor on behalf of the people. In Numbers 16:3-11, Korah thought that he could speak for Israel against Moses' pastoral authority, but he was strongly rebuked. He would later pay for his actions with his life, as well as with the lives of his family and everyone that followed him. It is dangerous for any member to line up with deacons against a God-sent leader. I have heard of deacons leading groups against their pastors, and then organizing churches. I contend that this is an abomination to the Lord.

This type of mentality in the church will not foster church growth, as we continue to progress through the new millennium. As the church confronts the rapid and complex transformations that are ushering us into the twenty-first century, many established churches and traditional deacon's ministries find themselves teetering between ineffectiveness and extinction. The reality is that they must change to meet the challenges of the present and upcoming generation, and they must do so quickly. Many deacons don't want to change, and many pastors don't want to upset the status quo. Change can come to churches by gently and positively helping them diagnose their true condition, and by pointing the way to a prescription. Every church situation is different, and the changes needed are as diverse as each congregation. Good church leaders, like good physicians, are careful to determine the correct diagnosis as well as prescription, while recognizing that each ministry has the power to change.[89]

I contend that deacons must change traditional mindsets and meet the relevant needs of the congregation with a servants attitude rather than a boss mentality. We must strive to have an effective deacon's ministry and not a dead, hard, stiff deacon's board. Effective deacon's ministries will focus on evangelism. The evangelistic task should first send us back to our Bibles. Careful, prayerful study of God's word will uncover the heart of His message and reveal it to an unbelieving world; it also will mean the recovery of the biblical priority of evangelism. Sad to say, evangelism in many churches today and for many individual Christians, seems almost an afterthought to the normal workings of the congregation or denomination.

Even a casual inspection of the New Testament will reveal that evangelism was the priority of the early church. Christians are called by God to do many things, but a church that has lost sight of the priority of evangelism has lost sight of its primary calling under God.

The recovery of the priority of evangelism should not lead us, however, to make a false distinction between the proclamation of the Gospel and social concerns. Both are part of God's calling and must go hand-in-hand. A Christian who fails to express Christ's love for humanity through clear verbal witness is also not living a life of full discipleship. Jesus, we read, "went through all the towns and villages, teaching in their synagogues, preaching the good news of the kingdom and healing every disease and sickness" (Matthew 9:35). Immediately afterwards, he commissioned the twelve disciples to go out and do likewise.

Deacon's Role in Evangelism

It is important that deacons be trained in how to lead others to Christ. One of the mission goals of the church is to evangelize; therefore, we must know how to <u>Biblically</u> lead others to Christ. Deacons must be knowledgeable of how one becomes saved (Romans 10:9-20; Acts 16:32); the need for salvation (Romans 3:23; 6:23); and God's desire for man (2 Peter 3:9; John 3:16; Romans 5:8). Some obstacles can get in the way of deacons being effective witnesses. Fear is natural because witnessing makes a person vulnerable. Therefore, deacons must have a hunger to see people saved--that must be more important than pride or hurt feelings. Lack of sensitivity can be an obstacle in deacon witnessing. Allow God to make you aware of those around you who need to learn of His love and grace. Don't let your self-reliance be a hindrance in witnessing. Remember, God is at work within you to speak to the unsaved. He often uses our weaknesses, not our strengths, to reach the lost. Therefore, do not think you have to be perfect and rely totally upon your own ability.

It is vitally important that deacons pray for the unsaved. Pray that God will save them and use you to bring sinners into the kingdom. If you know an unsaved person by name, pray for them by name. Deacons should set aside time everyday to pray for the lost. Learn to share what God has done (and is doing) for you. By doing so, people learn to identify with your testimony and God is honored. Personal testimonies have authority and can be used in many different situations. Every Christian has something to share.

Deacon's Role in Worship

Worship is an end in itself; it is not a means to something else. Church worship is the Opus Dei (the work of God), which is carried out for its own sake. Deacons must understand that they worship God purely for the sake of worshipping God.[90] They must ask themselves: "Do I worship when I lead worship?" To worship is to quicken the conscience by the holiness of God; to feed the mind with the truth of God; to purge the imagination by the beat of God; to open the heart to the love of God; and to devote the will to the purpose of God. Deacons have responsibilities in leading worship. In most churches, deacons are responsible for the devotional period of praise and worship. They should know who will help receive the offering and who will assist during the invitation. It would also be helpful to any pastor if deacons would stay awake during the preaching and bear witness to the word of God.

An Effective Deacon's Ministry

An effective deacon's ministry does not happen overnight. One must function and plan for effective ministry. Just because you have enough deacons to meet the congregation's needs is no guarantee that you are being effective. Pastors cannot achieve great leadership without effective delegation. Good leadership always includes some delegation. A congregation will respect the leadership that presents a plan to meet their needs. The deacons work with not only the pastor, but the pew also. He/She is chosen to live in relationships. They talk with God. They minister to their church. They support their pastor. They share with one another. As deacons come alive for Christ, the entire church will receive new incentive to open the Bible, with fresh vision; pray with more integrity; worship with more vitality; contribute more; and fully consecrate their lives in the service of the Lord.

Living Under the Lordship of Christ

The deacon-servant must acknowledge two basic elements of Christalogy. The first is Jesus is the savior of humankind. Jesus is Lord of all for all time. We do not make Christ Lord--He is Lord.[91] An effective deacon's ministry will operate under the Lordship of Christ. The key to any spiritual service is availability to God.

> I beseech you therefore, brethren; by the mercies of God, that ye present your bodies a living sacrifice, Holy acceptable unto God, which is your reasonable service. (Romans 12:1)

It is your availability, and not your ability, that allows God to be Lord of your life and of the church's ministries. When deacons come to meetings recognizing that He is Lord, they leave their agenda at home and allow God's agenda, through the shepherd/visionary, to take precedence. The only person who fears the will of God is the person who does not truly love and trust God. There is never a need to argue, fight, backbite, scheme or double-talk if you really want the will of God to be accomplished in the church. Just pray that God will speak to the pastor and give you spiritual eyes to see His will being accomplished.

Commitment to the Church

Being a deacon is not just about holding a glorified position. The office helps to provide members with positive examples of faithful Christians. The deacon (servant) should strive for personal commitment to the ongoing mandate of the church. The church is the continuation of the mind, message, mission and ministry of Jesus Christ.[92] Deacons should know that unless they are committed, they can be removed. The African American Church proves that just as the congregation can dismiss a pastor, so they can remove an entire deacon group. When deacons no longer serve their office with honor and distinction, they should be removed from office. Commitment is continual. I'm reminded of a friend, Reverend Eddie Hunter, pastor of the Miracle Baptist Church, Alexander City, Ala., who said, "Deacons are more concerned about being celebrities than they are about being servants." Celebrities shine in Hollywood, but only a servant shines in the kingdom. Deacons ought to be so committed to Christ that they have no problem being committed to the church.

CONCLUSION

Deacons of today must prepare to face a growing church in this new millennium. They must understand that unless a church is biblically in order, it cannot grow. When the pastor is the divine overseer and deacons are their helpers, through servant leadership, biblical order has been achieved. The congregations are the followers that help implement the God-given vision. This is a new day. Churches are growing and pastors and being used mightily by the Holy Spirit. If only deacons would flow under the anointing of their leaders and establish a relationship with them! This is a team effort, and we all are on the same team. Pastors oversee the entire church (1 Peter 5:2).[93] They also oversee the deacons. Therefore, deacons are not independent of their own leadership. I must encourage pastors to regularly clarify the deacons' duties. Lack of clarification causes many deacon related problems. It should be understood that there is work to be done. There is no room for lazy persons in team ministry. The pastor's work is more diverse, and deacons need to understand and appreciate that their responsibilities are more limited. Deacons can, therefore, be more focused on serving the Lord's people. There must be good coordination between pastor and deacon so that there will be a smooth working relationship.[94] The journey toward successful ministry should be a joint effort on the part of the layperson and pastor. Together they should seek to minister to those who are in need. Team enthusiasm is the key to success in the ministry effort.[95]

The rapidly changing advances in the new millennium require fresh ways to perform ministry. Without creativity, imagination and a commitment to the future of your church, you will miss magnificent opportunities to impact the new century with the Gospel. I challenge pastors and deacons to **keep the door open to innovation.** Because change is ever present, why not stop resisting it and start using it. Observe and use trends in society to shape new ways to minister. Watch for changes in the way people view life and how they respond to the work of the church. Concentrate on keeping whatever you do Christ-centered and your mission rooted in New Testament teaching. **We don't need to change the message but the method**. Pastor and deacon must admit that not everything is okay.[96] Many pastors would rarely admit that their deacon's ministry is not okay; but, for the most part, deacons think that everything is like it should be. I understand it is difficult for us to acknowledge failure in the church and failure in our area of ministry. However, if we do, we are taking a giant step toward renewal. Let's admit that the church is not what it should be. It is not what it can be until we fall in biblical order as servant-leaders. The future of the church awaits us; a future that will not tolerate yesterday's church in today's world, let alone the world of tomorrow. The future is in the hands of the leaders. This is an hour of challenges and of promise. The choice before pastors and deacons of yesterday is either to continue with our present pattern and style of ministry or allow a fresh look to be taken at our roles. This look is a reformation of the released power of God in the lives of those that want to please Him. God has given us instruction on how to conduct our lives in an effective and orderly fashion. As Scripture commands us, "Let all things be done decently and in order" (1 Corinthians 14:40).

ABOUT THE AUTHOR

Reverend Dr. John H. Walker

John H. Walker was born to the late Leforice Walker, Sr. and Inez Walker in Coosa County, Alabama. He attended the public schools in Coosa County and graduated from Goodwater High School. Dr. Walker has been married for the past twenty-two years to the former Rosie Knight. They have a daughter, Janetta Olivia, age fourteen and a son, John II, age eight.

Dr. Walker was brought under conviction by the Holy Spirit and accepted Christ as his personal Savior in 1978, while serving in the armed forces. On March 18, 1981, he was called into the Gospel ministry and licensed to preach by the New Light Baptist Church. He earned a Bachelor of Arts Degree from Shaw University and a Master of Divinity Degree from Shaw Divinity School, Raleigh, North Carolina, graduating Magna Cum Laude both times. He was the valedictorian of his graduating class at Greensboro Bible College, where he received a Theological and a Bible Degree.

Dr. Walker earned his Doctor of Ministry in Christian Leadership from Gordon Conwell Theological Seminary, in May of 1999, and is presently the first Vice Moderator of the Mecklenburg General Baptist Association. He is a certified instructor for the Southern Baptist Seminary Extension Program and teaches at Metrolina Seminary, Charlotte, NC, an extension of the Interdenominational Theological Center, Atlanta, Ga. He is also an adjunct professor at Shaw University Cape Center, Kannapolis, NC. Presently he is an instructor for the National Baptist Congress of Christian Education Convention.

After being led by the Holy Spirit, Dr. Walker prayerfully accepted the call as Pastor of Macedonia Baptist Church in Charlotte, NC, in March of 1992. Under the leadership of Pastor Walker, Macedonia has increased its membership and grown astronomically. More than forty-five ministries have been initiated under his leadership, such as Radio Broadcast Ministry, Friends Ministry, Sunday School Promotion Criteria, Security Ministry, Armorbearers, Wednesday Midday "Hour of Power," Youth Church, Hot Lunch Program (daily lunch for seniors), Wednesday Word with Full Worship, Drama Ministry, Tape Ministry, Youth Bible Study, Meals on Wheels Ministry, Prison Ministry, Leadership Seminar Training, Leadership Development Training, Men of Zion, Women's Prayer Ministry, Summer Youth Enrichment Camp, Deliverance Prayer, Christian Education Institute and Television Broadcast.

He is the author of *The Role of the Church in The Reclaiming of The Black Male*. Dr. Walker has been called upon frequently to develop seminars, instruct convention courses and lecture. He is a visionary leader for such a time as this.

ENDNOTES

1. Benjamin S. Baker, *Shepherding the Sheep* (Nashville: Broadman Press, 1983), p. 29.

2. Ibid., p. 41.

3. Lloyd Perry, *Getting the Church on Target* (Chicago: Moody, 1977), pp. 111-113.

4. Ibid., p. 36.

5. T. Dewitt Smith, *Putting Laypeople to Work* (Atlanta: Hope Publishing House, 1989), p. 22.

6. T. Dewitt Smith, *The Deacon in the Black Baptist Church* (U.S.A.: Church Town Productions, 1983), p. 13.

7. Rev. R. L. White Jr., *The Preacher Deacon Dilemma* (Nashville: National Baptist Publishing Board, 1993), p. 16.

8. Ibid., p. 17.

9. John C. Maxwell, *Developing the Leaders Around You* (Nashville: Thomas Nelson Publishers, 1995), p. 17.

10. Smith, *Putting Laypeople to Work*, p. 17.

11. Baker, *Shepherding the Sheep*, p. 18.

12. George McCalep, *Faithful Over a Few Things* (Lithonia, Ga.: Orman Press, 1996), p. 17.

13. Ibid.

14. Myles Munroe, *Becoming A Leader* (Nassau, Bahamas: Pneuma Life, 1993), p. 17.

15. Ibid., p. 8.

16. Ibid.

17. Ibid., p. 9.

18. Ibid., p. 12.

19. Smith, *Putting Laypeople to Work*, p. 4.

20. Floyd Massey Jr., and Samuel Berry McKinney, *Church Administration in the Black Perspective*, (Valley Forge, Pa.: Judson Press, 1976), p. 28.

21. H. L. King, *Who are Deacons According to the Bible, to the Church and to the Pastor* (LaGrange, Ga.: Judson Press, 1999), p. 4.

22. Ibid.

23. Henri Noumen, *The Wounded Healer* (Garden City, N.Y.: Doubleday & Co., 1972), pp. 19-21.

24. Wayne Goodwin: Lecture Notes, "Paradigms on Leadership," Doctor of Ministry Program, Gordon-Conwell, Charlotte, NC, 1996, p. 7.

25. Paul Tillich, *The New Being* (New York: Charles Scribner's Sons, 1955), p. 5.

26. Richard H. Niebuhr, *The Purpose of the Church and It's Ministry* (New York: Harper & Brothers,1956), p. 64.

27. Ibid.

28. Goodwin, pg. 15.

29. Ibid.

30. *The New Baptist Hymnal.* (Nashville: National Baptist Publishing Board, 1977), p. 138.

31. William E. Hull, *The Christian Experience of Salvation* (Nashville: Broadman Press, 1987), p. 135.

32. Ibid., p. 136

33. Ibid.

34. Goodwin, p. 15.

35. Ibid., p. 21.

36. Ibid., p. 15.

37. Rodney Ryce, *To the Deacon* (LaGrange, Ga.: Christian Goldmine Plus, 1995), p. 46.

38. Ibid.

39. Ibid., p. 47.

40. Ibid., p. 48.

41. Ibid.

42. Ibid.

43. Ibid., p. 50.

44. Ibid., p. 51.

45. Ibid., p. 26.

46. Ibid., p. 27.

47. Alexander Strauch, *The New Testament Deacon* (Littleton, Colo.: Lewis and Roth Publishers, 1992), p. 94.

48. Ibid.

49. Ibid.

50. Ibid.

51. Ibid., p. 56.

52. Ibid.

53. Augustine Confessions, *Book Seven--A.D. 397* (Kansas City: Sheed & Ward, 1943), chap. 21.

54. T. Dewitt Smith, Jr., *The Deacon in the Black Church*, (U.S.A.: Church/Town Productions, 1983), p. 22

55. Benjamin S. Baker, *Shepherding The Sheep* (Nashville: Broadman Press, 1983), p. 18.

56. Ibid, p. 19.

57. Ibid, p. 20.

58. Ibid, p. 21.

59. Ibid, p. 26.

60. Ibid, pp. 23-24.

61. Richard Dehaan, *Your Pastor and You* (Grand Rapids: Radio Bible Class, 1998), pp. 3-27.

62. T. Dewitt Smith, *The Deacon in the Black Baptist Church*, p. 13.

63. Ibid., p. 14.

64. Ibid., p. 17.

65. Charles E. Mainous, *What on Earth is A Deacon* (LaGrange, Ga.: The Christian Goldmine, 1971), p. 6.

66. Smith, *The Deacon in the Black Baptist Church*, p. 22.

67. Howard B. Foushee, *The Ministry of The Deacon* (Nashville: Convention Press, 1968), p. 17.

68. Smith, *The Deacon in the Black Baptist Church*, p. 23.

69. Ibid., p. 95.

70. Ibid., p. 42.

71. Ibid., p. 44.

72. Ibid., p. 45.

73. Ibid., p. 46.

74. Ibid., p. 50.

75. Ibid., p. 51.

76. Foushee, p. 30.

77. Richard Dehann, p. 19.

78. Ibid., p. 12.

79. Eric A. Mayes, Jr., *Deacon Training in the Black Church* (Oklahoma City: Beam Ministries, Inc., 1990), p. 100.

80. Mainous, p. 28.

81. Ibid., p. 29.

82. Ibid.

83. George McCalep, *Sin in the House* (Lithonia, Ga.: Orman Press, 1997), p. 36.

84. Ryce, Rodney, *To The Deacon* (San Jose, Calif: Color Connection, 1995), p. 70.

85. Ibid., p. 71.

86. Ibid., p. 80.

87. Ibid., p. 81.

88. Ibid.

89. Leith Anderson, *A Church for the 21st Century* (New York: Bethany House Publishers, 1992), p. 2.

90. Franklin M. Segler, *Christian Worship* (Nashville: Broadman Press, 1967), p. 4.

91. John MacArthur, *The Gospel According to Jesus* (Grand Rapids: Zondervan, 1988), p. 28.

92. T. Dewitt Smith, *New Testament Deacon in the African American Church* (Atlanta: Hope Publishing House, 1994), p. 9.

93. Gary L. Harbaugh, *Pastor as Person* (Minneapolis: Augsbury Press, 1989), p. 7.

94. Alexander Strauch, p. 78.

95. H. B. London, Jr. & Neil B. Wiseman, *The Heart of a Great Pastor* (Grands Rapids: Zondervan Publishing House, 1973), pp. 38-39.

96. Ibid.

BIBLIOGRAPHY

Anderson, Leith, *A Church for the 21st Century*. New York: Bethany House Publishers, 1992.

Augustine Confessions, *Book Seven--A.D. 397*. Kansas City: Sheed & Ward, 1943.

Baker, Benjamin S., *Shepherding the Sheep*. Nashville: Broadman Press, 1983.

Deweese, Charles W., *The Emerging Role of Deacons*. Nashville: Broadman Press, 1979.

Foushee, Howard B., *The Ministry of The Deacon*. Nashville: Convention Press, 1968.

Goodwin, Wayne: Lecture Notes, "Paradigms on Leadership." Doctor of Ministry Program, Gordon-Conwell, Charlotte, NC, 1998.

Harbaugh, Gary L., *Pastor as Person*. Minneapolis: Augsbury Press, 1989.

Hull, Williams E., *The Christian Experience of Salvation*. Nashville: Broadman Press, 1987.

King, H. L., *Who are Deacons According to the Bible, Church and to the Pastor*. LaGrange, Ga.: Christian Goldmine Plus, 1999.

Lloyd Perry, *Getting the Church on Target*. Chicago: Moody, 1977.

London Jr., H.B. and Neil B. Wiseman, *The Heart of a Great Pastor*. Grand Rapids: Zondervan Publishing House, 1984.

MacArthur, John, *The Gospel According to Jesus*. Grand Rapids: Zondervan Publishing House, 1988.

Mainous, Charles E., *What on Earth is a Deacon*. LaGrange, Ga.: The Christian Goldmine, 1971.

Massey, Jr., Floyd and Samuel Berry McKinney, *Church Administration in the Black Perspective*. Valley Forge, Pa.: Judson Press, 1976.

Mayes, Jr., Eric A., *Deacon Training in the Black Baptist Church*. Oklahoma City: Beam Ministries, Inc., 1990.

Maxwell, John C., *Developing The Leaders Around You*. Nashville: Thomas Nelson Publishers, 1995.

McCalep, George, *Faithful Over a Few Things*. Lithonia, Ga.: Orman Press, Inc., 1996.

--------------------, *Sin in The House*. Lithonia, Ga.: Orman Press, Inc., 1999.

Munroe, Myles, *Becoming a Leader*. Nassau, Bahamas: Pneuma Life, 1993.

Nichols, Harold, *The Work of the Deacon and Deaconess*. Valley Forge, Penn.: Judson Press, 1964.

Neibuhr, Richard H., *The Purpose of the Church and its Ministry*. New York: Harper & Brothers, 1956.

Nourmen, Henri, *The Wounded Healer*. Garden City, NY: Doubleday & Co., 1972.

Ryce, Rodney, *To The Deacon*. San Jose: Color Connection, 1995.

Segler, Franklin M., *Christian Worship*. Nashville: Broadman Press, 1967.

Sheffield, Robert, *Deacons as Leaders*. Nashville: Convention Press, 1991.

Smith Jr., T. Dewitt, *The Deacon in the Black Baptist Church*. U.S.A.: Church Town Productions, 1983.

----------------------, *Putting Laypeople to Work*. Atlanta: Hope Publishing House, 1989.

Strauch, Alexander, *The New Testament Deacon*. Littleton, Colo.: Lewis and Roth Publishers, 1992.

The New Baptist Hymnal, Nashville: National Baptist Publishing Board, 1977.

Tillich, Paul., *The New Being*. New York: Lewis and Roth Publishers, 1955.

Webb, Henry, *Deacons: Servant - Models in the Church*. Nashville: Convention Press, 1980.

White, Rev. R.L., *The Preacher Deacon Dilemma*. Nashville: National Baptist Publishing Board, 1993.

For Additional Information/Reorder
704-392-8496
Dr. John H. Walker
P. O. Box 217256
Charlotte, NC 28221-7256

TO SCHEDULE SEMINARS/WORKSHOPS
Contact Veronica Briscoe
(704) 392-8496